PAUL CUFFE

PAUL CUFFE

Arthur Diamond

Senior Consulting Editor
Nathan Irvin Huggins
Director
W.E.B. Du Bois Institute for Afro-American Research
Harvard University

CHELSEA HOUSE PUBLISHERS
New York   Philadelphia

Frontispiece: *The harbor at Freetown in Sierra Leone.*

CHELSEA HOUSE PUBLISHERS
Editor-in-Chief Nancy Toff
Executive Editor Remmel T. Nunn
Managing Editor Karyn Gullen Browne
Copy Chief Juliann Barbato
Picture Editor Adrian G. Allen
Art Director Maria Epes
Manufacturing Manager Gerald Levine

Black Americans of Achievement
Senior Editor Richard Rennert

Staff for PAUL CUFFE
Associate Editor Perry King
Copy Editor Brian Sookram
Deputy Copy Chief Ellen Scordato
Editorial Assistant Jennifer Trachtenberg
Picture Researcher Amla Sanghvi
Assistant Art Director Loraine Machlin
Designer Ghila Krajzman
Production Coordinator Joseph Romano
Cover Illustration Bill Donahey

First Printing

1 3 5 7 9 8 6 4 2

Library of Congress Cataloging-in-Publication Data

Diamond, Arthur.
  Paul Cuffe / Arthur Diamond.
    p. cm.—(Black Americans of achievement)
  Bibliography: p.
  Includes index.
  Summary: A biography of the American seaman and
merchant who encouraged fellow blacks to colonize Sierra
Leone, who sought a stronger legal position for blacks in
America, and who was responsible for a Massachusetts law
giving blacks the right to vote.
  ISBN 1-55546-579-X.
      0-7910-0236-5 (pbk.)
    1. Cuffe, Paul, 1759–1817—Juvenile literature.
2. Afro-Americans—Biography—Juvenile literature.
3. Afro-Americans—Massachusetts—Biography—Juvenile
literature. 4. Massachusetts—Biography—Juvenile literature. 5. Back to Africa movement—Juvenile literature.
6. Afro-Americans—Colonization—Sierra Leone—Juvenile
literature. 7. Sierra Leone—History—To 1896—Juvenile
literature. [1. Cuffe, Paul, 1759–1817. 2. Afro-Americans—Biography.] I. Title. II. Series.
E185.97.C96D53 1989
973.4'092'4—dc 19   89-757
[B]   CIP
[92]   AC

CONTENTS

—— ❦ ——

BLACK
AMERICANS
OF
ACHIEVEMENT

---❦---

MUHAMMAD ALI
heavyweight champion

RICHARD ALLEN
*founder of the
African Methodist
Episcopal church*

LOUIS ARMSTRONG
musician

JAMES BALDWIN
author

BENJAMIN BANNEKER
*scientist and
mathematician*

MARY MCLEOD BETHUNE
educator

BLANCHE K. BRUCE
politician

RALPH BUNCHE
diplomat

GEORGE WASHINGTON CARVER
botanist

CHARLES WADDELL CHESTNUTT
author

PAUL CUFFE
merchant and abolitionist

FREDERICK DOUGLASS
abolitionist editor

CHARLES R. DREW
physician

W. E. B. DUBOIS
educator and author

PAUL LAURENCE DUNBAR
poet

DUKE ELLINGTON
bandleader and composer

RALPH ELLISON
author

ELLA FITZGERALD
singer

MARCUS GARVEY
black-nationalist leader

PRINCE HALL
social reformer

WILLIAM H. HASTIE
educator and politician

MATTHEW A. HENSON
explorer

CHESTER HIMES
author

BILLIE HOLIDAY
singer

JOHN HOPE
educator

LENA HORNE
entertainer

LANGSTON HUGHES
poet

JAMES WELDON JOHNSON
author

SCOTT JOPLIN
composer

MARTIN LUTHER KING, JR.
civil rights leader

JOE LOUIS
heavyweight champion

MALCOLM X
militant black leader

THURGOOD MARSHALL
Supreme Court justice

ELIJAH MUHAMMAD
religious leader

JESSE OWENS
champion athlete

GORDON PARKS
photographer

SIDNEY POITIER
actor

ADAM CLAYTON POWELL, JR.
political leader

A. PHILIP RANDOLPH
labor leader

PAUL ROBESON
singer and actor

JACKIE ROBINSON
baseball great

JOHN RUSSWURM
publisher

SOJOURNER TRUTH
antislavery activist

HARRIET TUBMAN
antislavery activist

NAT TURNER
slave revolt leader

DENMARK VESEY
slave revolt leader

MADAME C. J. WALKER
entrepreneur

BOOKER T. WASHINGTON
educator

WALTER WHITE
political activist

RICHARD WRIGHT
author

ON
ACHIEVEMENT

———— ❧ ————

Coretta Scott King

Before you begin this book, I hope you will ask yourself what the word excellence means to you. I think that it's a question we should all ask, and keep asking as we grow older and change. Because the truest answer to it should never change. When you think of excellence, perhaps you think of success at work; or of becoming wealthy; or meeting the right person, getting married, and having a good family life.

Those important goals are worth striving for, but there is a better way to look at excellence. As Martin Luther King, Jr., said in one of his last sermons, "I want you to be first in love. I want you to be first in moral excellence. I want you to be first in generosity. If you want to be important, wonderful. If you want to be great, wonderful. But recognize that he who is greatest among you shall be your servant."

My husband, Martin Luther King, Jr., knew that the true meaning of achievement is service. When I met him, in 1952, he was already ordained as a Baptist preacher and was working towards a doctoral degree at Boston University. I was studying at the New England Conservatory and dreamed of accomplishments in music. We married a year later, and after I graduated the following year we moved to Montgomery, Alabama. We didn't know it then, but our notions of achievement were about to undergo a dramatic change.

You may have read or heard about what happened next. What began with the boycott of a local bus line grew into a national movement, and by the time he was assassinated in 1968 my husband had fashioned a black movement powerful enough to shatter forever the practice of racial segregation. What you may not have read about is where he got his method for resisting injustice without compromising his religious beliefs.

He adopted the strategy of nonviolence from a man of a different race, who lived in a distant country, and even practiced a different religion. The man was Mahatma Gandhi, the great leader of India, who devoted his life to serving humanity in the spirit of love and nonviolence. It was in these principles that Martin discovered his method for social reform. More than anything else, those two principles were the key to his achievements.

This book is about black Americans who served society through the excellence of their achievements. It forms a part of the rich history of black men and women in America—a history of stunning accomplishments in every field of human endeavor, from literature and art to science, industry, education, diplomacy, athletics, jurisprudence, even polar exploration.

Not all of the people in this history had the same ideals, but I think you will find something that all of them have in common. Like Martin Luther King, Jr., they all decided to become "drum majors" and serve humanity. In that principle—whether it was expressed in books, inventions, or song—they found something outside themselves to use as a goal and a guide. Something that showed them a way to serve others, instead of living only for themselves.

Reading the stories of these courageous men and women not only helps us discover the principles that we will use to guide our own lives but also teaches us about our black heritage and about America itself. It is crucial for us to know the heroes and heroines of our history and to realize that the price we paid in our struggle for equality in America was dear. But we must also understand that we have gotten as far as we have partly because America's democratic system and ideals made it possible.

We are still struggling with racism and prejudice. But the great men and women in this series are a tribute to the spirit of our democratic ideals and the system in which they have flourished. And that makes their stories special and worth knowing. ◂◦▸

PAUL CUFFE

1
TO BUILD
A SCHOOLHOUSE

ONE MORNING IN 1797, Paul Cuffe, a prosperous merchant and sea captain, walked briskly from his farm to the nearby town of Westport, Massachusetts, brimming with excitement at the plan he was about to discuss with the townspeople. Westport did not have a public school at that time. A formal education was available to the local children only if their parents were willing to send them to school in a neighboring village.

Cuffe had seven children of his own, and he was determined that they be educated in a classroom close to their home. Accordingly, he wanted to ask the people of Westport to help him build a schoolhouse. He was sure that the villagers would see the wisdom of his proposal and would agree to work with him to make it a reality. If everybody in the community pitched in to help raise the building's walls, he calculated that the schoolhouse could be erected within a week.

Cuffe had reason to be optimistic that his proposal would meet with acceptance. At the age of 38, the strong and resourceful merchant was the owner of a thriving shipping business and was well on his way to becoming one of the first wealthy black men in

The town of Westport, Massachusetts, served as the home base of Cuffe's maritime trading operations. During the early 1800s, his trade network stretched from America to the coast of West Africa.

America. He walked to Westport with the vigor of someone who had complete faith in himself and his ability to get things done. In comparison with the hurdles he had already scaled—he had stood face to face with pirates and had run British blockades during the American Revolution—the founding of a school seemed to be a small task.

Cuffe went from door to door when he reached Westport, greeting the residents and telling them about his idea for a schoolhouse. He asked for their cooperation in the project, reminding them that their children should not be deprived of a good education. A self-taught man who was still only semiliterate, he tried to make the townspeople see that it was in their best interests to have their children learn the basics of reading, writing, and arithmetic in a school of their own. If the town's children were given a good education, he said, there was no limit to what they could accomplish.

The replies that Cuffe received were all the same, but they were not the responses he had expected. No one agreed to help him build a schoolhouse. Some said they did not have the time to lend a hand. Others could not afford the expense. Cuffe was told by several people that the word of the Lord as written in the Bible was the only teaching their children needed. Everyone, it seemed, had an excuse.

Disappointed by the reception he was given in town, Cuffe made a circuit of the countryside and discussed his idea with a number of farming families. After hours of trudging down dirt roads and across cow pastures, he had to accept the truth: The farmers were no more enthusiastic about his plan than the townspeople were. Dismayed, he returned to his farm to ponder his predicament.

Why had the people of Westport given him such a cool response? Cuffe knew that the answer to this question had more to do with the color of his skin than with the merits of his proposal. In late 18th-century America, blacks were not regarded by whites as capable leaders. Cuffe's neighbors could not accept a black man guiding them to a better life, even if what he advised was simple to accomplish and made perfect sense. Neither did the people of Westport find the idea of their children going to school with black children to be very agreeable.

Cuffe was hurt by his neighbors' refusal even though he was well aware of the racial views that prevailed in America. He had been living near Westport for many years and had been heavily involved in the community's affairs. His neighbors knew he was a man of good judgment and unusual boldness. The construction of his own shipyard and dock had shown them that he was someone who could get things done.

Yet the racial prejudice that Cuffe faced was deeply embedded in the fabric of American society. This was, after all, a time in which the life of most black Americans was dominated by the institution of slavery. Ninety percent of the country's nearly 1 million blacks were slaves, the majority of whom toiled on farms and plantations in the South. Slaves had no rights beyond what their masters chose to give them, and they were frequently treated with extreme brutality.

In the South, only a small number of slaves were ever granted their freedom. The situation was far better for blacks who lived in the North, where antislavery sentiment had gained a foothold. In fact, most northern states, including Massachusetts, had already outlawed slavery within their borders, and many northern cities had become home to growing communities of free blacks. Some enterprising black merchants and tradesmen, including Cuffe, even lived in relative comfort.

For the most part, though, free blacks did not own much property. Most were extremely poor and were shut out of all but the lowest-paying jobs.

A page from a letter copybook belonging to Cuffe's father, a self-taught man who noted his children's birth dates in this record. Even though Paul was never formally educated, he was anxious to have his own children attend a neighborhood school.

Treated as second-class citizens, they were generally excluded from many of the privileges enjoyed by other Americans, including the right to vote and the right to an education. The world they inhabited was generally far removed from the world of whites; indeed, they were forced to sit in separate sections from whites even in church.

Cuffe, a freeborn son of a former slave, had never allowed bigotry to get in his way. His right to pursue his livelihood as a shipowner and private businessman had often been challenged, but he had fought every step of the way with a quiet courage that earned him the respect of all who met him. To those who questioned his ability or character because of the color of his skin, he responded not with anger or defiance but with action.

The townspeople's rejection of his plan for a school did not deter Cuffe in the least. He had resolved that his children must be educated.

The local residents forgot about Cuffe's proposal in the days that followed his visit to Westport, and life there went on as usual. The villagers struggled to win a living from the land or the nearby waters, and the men gathered in taverns at the end of each workday to meet with friends and talk about local events.

As the weeks passed, one item of gossip kept creeping into their conversations: The black sea captain was erecting a new building on his farm. No one asked him what he was constructing, but the rumors about the new structure quickly multiplied: Some said it was a barn; others thought it was a warehouse. Perhaps a few suspected the truth, that Cuffe was building the school they had unanimously rejected.

The structure was completed after several months. Cuffe had planned the construction himself and had built the schoolhouse with his own funds. It stood at the edge of his property.

Cuffe's next step was to advertise for a teacher. As soon as he found a suitable person, the school-

Although most northern states had abolished slavery by the beginning of the 19th century, free blacks and fugitive slaves lived in constant fear of being kidnapped and sold into slavery in the South. Slave hunters, also known as blackbirders, often abducted suspected runaways and brought them to slave territories.

house was ready to open. His children were about to receive the education he had planned for them.

But Cuffe had not built the schoolhouse for his children alone. He went again to town, this time to offer his neighbors free use of the school. Unlike his earlier visit to Westport, this time the townspeople listened attentively to what he had to say, and most of them accepted his offer.

Cuffe watched on the first day of classes as his children walked alongside the white children of Westport and entered the new school. "I feel to encourage the preparation of young men of color fit for usefulness," he would later write to a friend. "It will be a convincing prop to those who show to them in utter abhorrence that they are not capable of mental endowments." He knew that an education was the key to enabling blacks to demonstrate that they had the same "mental endowments" as whites.

The building, which was known as Cuff's School, proved to be extremely well constructed, and it remained the town's only schoolhouse for a long while. By the time another school was erected many years later, Cuffe had begun to search in Africa for a new homeland for his oppressed black countrymen—a place, he said, where black Americans could "rise to be a people." During this quest, he convened with presidents and powerful politicans and dined with some of the richest men in America. Yet he never allowed his own good fortune to sidetrack him from trying to realize his grandest of dreams. In small ways and large, he always let it be known that racial equality could be won with courage and determination—and by refusing to take no for an answer. ◆

Cuffe passed on his business knowledge and navigational skills to his children after they were educated at the school he built in Westport. This page, with its drawings of a building and a ship, is taken from his personal journal.

2

THE RIGHTS OF
A FREE MAN

Paul Cuffe (pronounced CUFF-ee) was born on Cuttyhunk Island off the southern coast of Massachusetts in 1759. His birthplace, the westernmost of the Elizabeth Islands, is a bare, rocky place that provides little shelter or arable land. But the island's rough features have often prompted its residents to cultivate a strong, resourceful spirit. Paul's African-born father and Native American mother were resilient people, and Paul became one as well.

Paul's father, Cuffe Slocum, was a member of the powerful Ashanti tribe of West Africa; his tribal name, Kofi, means "born on Friday." His youth in Africa was cut short, however, when, at the age of 10, he was captured by slavers and put on board a ship to America.

Cuffe Slocum's tragic fate was shared by millions of other Africans between the 15th and 19th centuries. During this period, European nations raided Africa for a cheap source of labor for their colonies in the New World. The captives were often the leading members of their tribe: princes, priests, merchants, and warriors who were sold into slavery after their tribe was defeated in battle. The captives were sometimes forced to march as many as 500 miles to

Slave ships were a common sight along the African coasts from the 15th century until the mid-1800s, when the slave trade came to an end. Cuffe's father was among the millions of Africans sold to white slavers and transported to North and South America.

17

Africa's west coast, where the slave depots were located.

Once the slaves were aboard a ship, they were herded beneath the decks and packed in storage holds that were usually just 18 inches high. There each slave was chained, often by the neck and legs, and was wedged against another captive. With so little air in the holds, the captives were constantly laboring to breathe during the nightmarish trip across the Atlantic Ocean. As a result, many slaves died during the voyage; their bodies were thrown overboard—so many, in fact, that sharks were said to follow the ships all the way from Africa to America.

Cuffe Slocum was a strong young man. He survived the journey and was sold to Ebenezer Slocum, a ship's captain from the coastal town of Dartmouth, Massachusetts. As was the custom of the times, Cuffe took his master's last name for his own.

After working for his owner for 15 years, Cuffe Slocum was sold by Ebenezer Slocum to his nephew, John Slocum. Cuffe Slocum was fortunate that neither of his masters abused their slaves; some owners administered regular lashings with a whip, followed by a washing-down with cold, stinging brine. John Slocum, in fact, made an agreement with his new slave: Cuffe Slocum would be allowed to manumit himself—he could buy his freedom—if he did extra work for his master. In 1745, less than three years after becoming John Slocum's slave, the hardworking Cuffe Slocum became a free man.

After gaining his freedom, Cuffe Slocum met and became engaged to Ruth Moses, an American Indian from nearby Cuttyhunk Island. He married her in 1746 and immediately set about looking for a place to raise a family. At the time, the majority of the freed slaves in America lived in cities. The largest communities were in Baltimore, Philadelphia, and New York. Most of these free blacks led a hand-to-mouth existence and lived in hovels on narrow, dirty streets.

Cuffe Slocum, wanting a better kind of environment for himself and his wife, elected to move to Cuttyhunk Island. There he and Ruth lived with her family, who were Gay Head Indians, part of the once mighty Wampanoag tribe of southern Massachusetts. The Wampanoag, who called themselves the "First People," had befriended the Pilgrims of Plymouth Colony in 1620 and had helped the ill-prepared English settlers survive their first winter in America by teaching them how to grow corn, pumpkins, and cranberries, and how to hunt wild turkeys.

Dated 1742, this bill of sale for Cuffe Slocum, the slave who later became Paul's father, was the first documentation of the Cuffe family in America. A highly skilled laborer, Slocum was eventually freed by his master.

Years later, as the English settlements in Massachusetts expanded, the good relations between the Wampanoag and the Pilgrims began to fade. In 1675, hostilities boiled over after three Indians were executed at Plymouth Colony for an alleged murder. The Wampanoag were a proud people and were not afraid to fight back against the better-armed whites. Organizing under Metacomet, a Wampanoag chief who was known to whites as King Philip, the tribe attacked the white colonists. The valiant Metacomet was defeated and killed, however, and most of the Wampanoag were eventually driven out of southern New England.

The Indians who remained in Massachusetts found natural allies among the colony's black slaves, who were also victims of racial oppression, and marriages between the two groups were commonplace.

Cuffe's mother was a descendant of the Wampanoag Indians, a tribe that occupied much of Massachusetts when the Pilgrims arrived there in 1620. A half century later, the English colonists killed the Wampanoag's courageous leader, Metacomet, and expelled the tribe from its native lands.

Cuffe Slocum was welcomed into the society of the Gay Head Indians, and he and Ruth farmed and fished for a living. All told, they had 10 children: David, Jonathan, Sarah, Mary, Phebe, John, Paul, Lydia, Ruth, and Freelove. Paul was the youngest male in the household.

Surrounded by many supportive relatives on Cuttyhunk, the Slocum children belonged to a close-knit family that was proud of its Indian heritage. The tribe, according to Wampanoag legend, was protected by a powerful guardian, a giant named Maushop who was said to have hollowed out Buzzard's Bay—the body of water surrounded by Cuttyhunk and the four other Elizabeth Islands—one night in his sleep. On that same restless night, he had gotten sand in his moccasins and had emptied them, thereby forming two large islands: Nantucket Island and Martha's Vineyard.

Cuffe Slocum, who was skilled in carpentry and other building and hauling trades, developed a small but thriving business that served the residents of Westport, Dartmouth, New Bedford, and other towns around Buzzard's Bay. He had also learned how to write—an unusual feat for a former slave—and kept a business ledger of his expenses and profits. As Paul and the other Slocum children grew older, they were brought into their father's business and were taught how to build a house, manage a farm, and navigate a fully loaded boat in treacherous coastal waters. They also learned the rudiments of reading and writing and were instructed in Quaker values of honesty, courtesy, thrift, and hard work. The Quakers, also known as the Society of Friends, have traditionally been pacifists, and in 18th-century America they were strong opponents of slavery.

As Cuffe Slocum's business prospered, he was able to afford better housing for his family. He moved them first to Martha's Vineyard and then to the main-

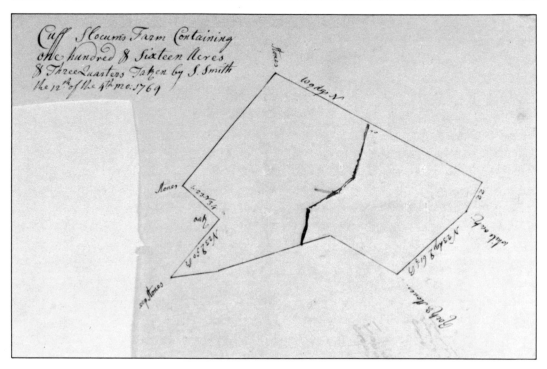

By the time this map of Cuffe Slocum's farm near Westport, Massachusetts, was drawn in 1769, the industrious tradesman and his family had built a large house and planted many acres of corn on their plot of land.

land, where, in 1766, he purchased a 120-acre farm near Westport. Paul, who was seven years old at the time, joined his brothers and sisters in helping to clear the land and to erect the family's impressive farmhouse. During the next five years, he saw his father's homestead thrive. But in 1772, the teenager suffered a shocking blow when his father died.

Cuffe Slocum had come to America in chains, yet he had managed to gain his liberty and had prospered as a free man, buying a huge tract of land that he left to his family. His legacy of hard work, persistence, and courage was complemented by the powerful sense of family fostered by his wife and her people. At the time of his father's death, 13-year-old Paul did not fully realize how strongly his family heritage had shaped his view of the world. But he did know that he no longer wanted to bear his father's slave name, and he changed his name to Paul Cuffe. Later on, his family members followed his example.

While other young men his age received school-ing or were apprenticing a trade, Paul remained at home with his widowed mother and helped his brother John manage the family farm. But as he plowed and planted, he also wondered about his fu-ture, and he soon decided that the sea was in his blood. Eager for adventure at age 14, he followed the example of many young men reared on the coast of New England: He went down to the bay, found a ship, and signed on as a crew member.

Paul's choice of a ship was characteristic of a daring young man. Instead of signing up with a cargo ship, he joined a whaling vessel. At that time, the ports of New England were becoming the centers of the hugely profitable whaling business, which pro-vided oil for lamps and tallow for candles. The life of a whaling man was extremely dangerous, however. When a whale was sighted, the sailors rowed out to

Merchants and seamen of differ-ent races conduct business at an early trading outpost in New Bed-ford, Massachusetts. During the 1700s, many small New England coastal towns became thriving centers of the whaling industry, which provided oil for lamps and bones for needles, combs, and other household products.

it in a small boat and attempted to embed a harpoon in the whale's back. A rope attached to the harpoon was also fastened to the boat, and the huge wounded mammal often dragged it for miles before dying. Sometimes, boats were crushed by the whale's powerful tail. But a successful hunt could make a shipowner very rich, and many seafarers were attracted to whaling ships because they offered higher wages than other types of vessels.

Cuffe spent much of his first voyage observing life on board a whaling ship. He also paid strict attention to the captain, who patiently taught the young black sailor the art of navigation. The whaling expedition clearly enthralled the youthful Cuffe: After his first stint at sea ended, he immediately signed up for another voyage.

On his second trip, Cuffe sailed on a cargo ship to the West Indies, the center of the international sugar trade. Millions of slaves were employed on these islands in the sugar fields of large plantations. Because it was cheaper to import new slaves than to provide proper food and medical care for the work force, the Africans brought to the Caribbean were literally worked to death.

Paul was stunned at the brutality of the slave system. He witnessed men and women being branded at slave markets and saw slaves being severely whipped when they tried to rest from their labors. The trip left the young black sailor with a deep revulsion for the slave trade and set him thinking about how this inhumane system could be stopped.

Cuffe's third voyage, also on board a cargo ship, began in 1776, a momentous time in American history. For many years, the American colonists had been growing increasingly angry that they had to pay taxes to Britain even though they were not allowed to have their own representatives in the British government. The dispute erupted into open warfare in

1775, and by July of the next year the colonists had declared their independence from Britain. The British immediately arranged their ships in a tight blockade of America's main ports while their army attempted to put down the rebellion.

The captain of Cuffe's ship attempted to sail through the British blockade. For three days, the ship averted the hostile warships, but it was finally spotted and seized by a British frigate. According to British law, sailors on enemy vessels could be commanded to join the British navy when their ships were captured. Paul and his shipmates were lined up on the deck of the frigate and were presented with a choice: either join the British forces or be thrown in prison. All of the colonial sailors chose imprisonment.

West Indian slaves are shown harvesting and processing cotton in an 18th-century illustration (the numbers demonstrate different steps of the manufacturing process). Cuffe sailed to the West Indies on one of his early voyages and was horrified to hear stories about the savage treatment of slaves on the islands' plantations.

Cuffe and his shipmates were sent to a prison in New York, then a thriving port city under British control. Soon after their arrival, the prisoners had an odd bit of luck. A fire destroyed many of the city's buildings, leaving few quarters for the wintering British troops. To make room for the soldiers, Paul and the others were set free.

Cuffe returned to the family farm near Westport and remained there for more than a year. As the American Revolution continued, the British attempted to enlist Indians and blacks in the Royal Army. Some slaves seized the opportunity to flee from their masters and take refuge among the British. But Paul already had his freedom, and he remained devoted to the patriotic cause.

When Cuffe finally returned to the sea, he sailed on board another cargo ship to the West Indies. Seeing again the horrors of the West Indian slave trade, he felt a strong desire to avoid all contact with

Cuffe was imprisoned in a New York jail for a few weeks in 1776, after his ship tried to run a British blockade at the start of the American Revolution. He and his fellow crewmen were released after much of the city's available housing was destroyed by fire.

the islands in the future. But a common seaman has little control over the destination of his ship, so Cuffe decided that to truly be his own master, he must go into business for himself.

In 1779, with the help of his brother David, Cuffe built a boat and began a small trading operation along the New England coast. He picked a good time to start his business because a British raid on the port of Dartmouth, Massachusetts, the year before had destroyed much of the area's shipping and opened up new opportunities for small traders. The Cuffe brothers made a handsome profit by running the British blockade to bring supplies to hard-pressed seaside communities.

Although the Cuffes managed to elude British patrols, they were not so lucky at escaping the attention of pirates who hid in the small bays and inlets of the New England shoreline. During one of their trips, the Cuffes were chased and seized by a pirate ship. Outnumbered, they could only stand by angrily as the thieves stripped their vessel of its cargo.

The encounter with the pirates made Paul more cautious, but it did not rob him of his desire to expand his shipping venture. David, however, decided that the business was too risky and bowed out of the partnership. Paul continued making the dangerous voyages by himself, and he soon established a trade with towns on the island of Nantucket.

But it was not enough for the 20-year-old black merchant to stay alert and watchful along the rocky New England coastline. A type of piracy threatened him on land, too. Only individuals who owned property were allowed the full rights of American citizenship, including the privileges of voting and holding public office. Furthermore, these rights were available only to whites. Blacks, Indians, and people of mixed blood were excluded from the political system. The tax collector, however, was color-blind, and Cuffe

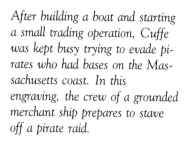

After building a boat and starting a small trading operation, Cuffe was kept busy trying to evade pirates who had bases on the Massachusetts coast. In this engraving, the crew of a grounded merchant ship prepares to stave off a pirate raid.

and other black men who owned property were supposed to pay a substantial sum to the Commonwealth of Massachusetts each year.

Cuffe was angered by the hypocrisy of the system. His countrymen were fighting to become independent from a government that taxed them without allowing them any political representation. Yet he, a respectable businessman who had spent time as a British prisoner of war, was denied the privileges that white citizens assumed were clearly theirs.

In 1780, Paul and John Cuffe and five other free blacks took action to change what they regarded as an unfair situation. They sent a petition to the council of Bristol County, their local legislative body, requesting to be exempted from all taxes. The document, though written in a sometimes halting style, clearly presented the case for the complainants. It read, in part, "We being chiefly of the African extraction . . . are not allowed the privilege of freemen of the state, having no vote or influence in the election with those that tax us."

Cuffe and the other petitioners waited anxiously for the response from the county council. When the answer to their plea arrived, John Cuffe recorded the disappointment in his journal. "But we received none," he said of their request for tax relief.

The days of distress had only just begun. The Cuffe brothers had been delinquent in paying their taxes, and they now owed taxes for three years, stretching back to 1778. Now, in the wake of their petition's failure, they faced prosecution for tax evasion. The amount they were assessed was huge, and they were unable to pay it.

Paul and John decided to try another tactic. Massachusetts law stated that Indians did not have to pay taxes. Accordingly, the brothers submitted another petition to the county council, this time emphasizing their Indian ancestry.

The second petition met with even less success than the first. On December 19, 1780, Cuffe answered a knock on his front door and was greeted by a group of county constables with orders to take him and John to prison. Their imprisonment lasted only a few hours, however. A sympathetic councilman named Walter Spooner was able to arrange their release until their case could be given a fair hearing.

Nevertheless, Paul remained outraged at the hypocrisy that was taking place. The hostility he felt from many of his neighbors did not make matters any better. In fact, he began to drink heavily to ease his anguish and eventually had to be taken in hand by John.

The Cuffes' tax-protest campaign continued into the spring and summer of 1781. Their cause was strengthened when the Massachusetts legislature issued a new state constitution that did not specifically

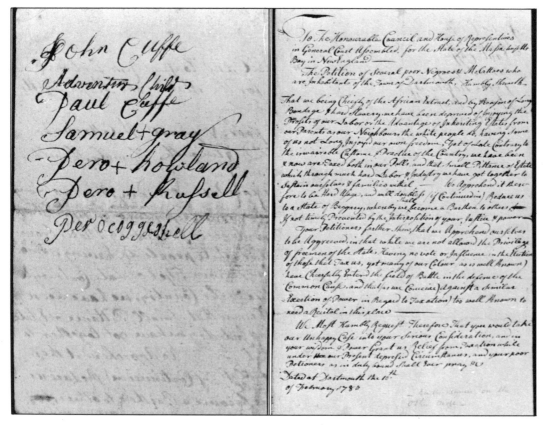

In 1780, Cuffe, his brother John, and five black neighbors petitioned the local county legislature in Massachusetts to exempt them from paying taxes until they were allowed the same voting rights as white citizens. The petitioners compared their own cause to that of the colonists' fight with Britain to end taxation without representation.

exclude blacks from voting, although town and county laws still effectively impeded blacks from exercising their voting rights. The Cuffes' case attracted a great deal of public debate, and their trial met many delays as the merits of their petition were argued. Finally, the weary council members agreed to accept a small tax payment from the brothers and dropped all other charges against them.

The tax-resistance campaign helped Paul realize that he might be able to bring about changes in society if he was willing to stand up to unfair laws. It also helped him understand that his black heritage linked him to all other blacks. Their struggle was one and the same.

The battle for racial justice had already achieved some success in Massachusetts. In 1777, a group of black men in Boston, led by community leader Prince Hall, had petitioned the Massachusetts legislature to abolish slavery in the Commonwealth. By 1783, their goal was achieved when Massachusetts's chief justice, William Cushing, granted a slave plaintiff named Quork Walker his freedom and ruled that slavery was forbidden by law. During that same year, the legislature passed a law declaring that taxpaying black property owners had the right to vote.

Two other events of great importance to Cuffe occurred in 1783. First, the Americans and the British signed a peace treaty confirming that the colonies were an independent nation; American seamen could finally raise their sails without fear of being confronted by the guns of a British warship. At the same time that his countrymen were celebrating their independence, Cuffe married Alice Pequit, who was of Wampanoag descent. With the conflicts of the last three years finally set aside, he could enjoy what promised to be more peaceful times with his wife and family. 🏵

3
THE AFRICAN CAPTAIN

THE QUARTER CENTURY that spanned the years 1780 to 1806 was largely a time of building for Paul Cuffe. Married and with a family to support, the shipping entrepreneur worked hard to make sure that his wife and children could live in comfort. With his steadily improving business acumen and his willingness to take risks to better his financial position, he was able to overcome many of the obstacles that confronted most black merchants.

Throughout this period, Cuffe not only looked after his wife and children but made sure that his brothers and sisters were provided for as well. He also became increasingly intent on helping out members of an even larger family—the blacks of Africa and the United States.

Cuffe's maritime holdings had humble origins, stretching back to the boat he and his brother David had constructed to run the British blockade during the war years. During the 1780s, he used the money he made from his trading ventures to build larger ships suitable for longer voyages. With his first ship, a small vessel of the schooner class, he went on short trading runs along the southern New England shoreline. He took his second ship, a slightly larger schooner, to

Cuffe's success on hazardous—but usually profitable—whaling expeditions in the years following the American Revolution allowed him to build a shipyard as well as a sizable fleet of vessels.

the waters around Newfoundland to fish for cod and salmon. In 1787, he purchased his third schooner, which he named the *Sunfish* in honor of the first fish caught in the ship's nets.

The success of Cuffe's shipping company was virtually unprecedented for a black-owned enterprise at that time. Aided by his business partner, his brother-in-law Michael Wainer, Cuffe proved that he could compete with white traders. The crews of the company's ships were composed entirely of blacks and Indians, including Wainer's six sons. With this unusual but well-trained group, Cuffe made many profitable voyages.

While captaining the *Sunfish* on a whaling expedition to Belle Isle Strait off the coast of Newfoundland, Cuffe had a chance to show his mettle. Having gone out with a crew of only 10 men and just 2 whale boats on board the ship, he was not especially well prepared to hunt the huge mammals. He had expected to meet up with other whaling ships and, as was the common practice, all of the vessels would work together. When he arrived at the strait, however, the captains of four other whaling ships refused to have anything to do with Cuffe and his black and Indian crew. They told him that the *Sunfish* would have to hunt by itself.

The captains of the other ships, expecting that Cuffe would give up and go home, became angry when he calmly stood by and waited for his quarry to appear. When the whales were finally sighted, Cuffe leaped into action and lowered a boat from the *Sunfish* to begin the hunt. Awed by the courage of the nonwhite crew and afraid that the whales might quickly disappear from the area, the other captains joined the hunt. Of the seven whales caught by the group, six were killed by the *Sunfish*, and Cuffe himself harpooned two. He sailed home with a rich cargo of oil.

Cuffe's response to the snub in the Belle Isle Strait was typical of the manner in which he conducted his business. Knowing that prejudice could not be overcome with harsh words and hostile actions, he resolved always to meet bigotry with a polite, cool, dignified response. He had learned that he could use his personal charm and his reputation for fair business dealing to earn the respect of many people who initially shunned him because of the color of his skin. His battle was for all blacks who wanted to succeed in business, and he was determined to show by example that blacks could be the equals of whites on the deck of a ship and in the marketplace of any seaport.

The first five vessels in Cuffe's fleet were schooners of the type shown here and were manned by all-black crews, a rare sight to onlookers in ports from Maryland to Nova Scotia.

The growth in Cuffe's shipping business was matched by the expansion of his household. By 1790, he and Alice had four daughters to raise: Naomi, Mary, Ruth, and Alice. Within the next nine years, Paul, Jr., Rhoda, and William were added to the family. The children grew up on the family's farm, which was located along the banks of the Acoaxet River in Westport.

By 1792, Cuffe owned two ships, the *Sunfish* and another schooner he named the *Mary* in honor of his sister, who had married Michael Wainer. Four years later, he took a huge gamble by selling both ships in order to pay for a new schooner, the large, fast *Ranger*. Cuffe was especially proud of this ship because it was the first to be built in his shipyard, which he had recently constructed beside his farm.

On his initial voyage aboard the *Ranger*, Cuffe went for the first time to the South. He had learned that he could find in Maryland a plentiful supply of corn to transport to New England. Accordingly, he sailed his ship down the narrow, winding Nanticoke River and docked at Vienna, Maryland.

The *Ranger*'s arrival caused a stir in the small slaveholding community. The townspeople had never seen a ship manned entirely by blacks before, and they were even more dumbstruck when they learned that the *Ranger*'s captain and owner was also black. Their surprise was accompanied by fear, because many people in Vienna believed that the visitor was a rebel ship whose mission was to arouse a revolt among the area's slaves. Fresh in their mind were the stories coming from a West Indian colony (now called Haiti) where slaves were engaged in a massive rebellion against their French rulers. Many of the town's residents wanted Cuffe and his crew to be ordered to leave.

Although Cuffe knew he was unwelcome, he refused to back down before a hostile public. He presented himself to Vienna's officials and showed them documents that proved he was a legitimate trader. The authorities realized there were no grounds for barring the *Ranger* from their town, and they reluctantly allowed the vessel to stay.

Cuffe immediately went to work to change the attitudes of the suspicious townspeople. Before long, they welcomed the courteous, charismatic captain and his friendly crew. Many came down to the dock to investigate Cuffe's remarkable ship. He was even invited to dine with one of the town's most prominent white families.

Cuffe eventually purchased a large amount of corn. After sailing home, he sold the cargo for a handsome profit. He later made another voyage for a second, equally profitable cargo.

In 1791, slaves in a West Indian colony rebelled against their French rulers and established the black republic of Haiti. Cuffe's ship subsequently aroused fears when it sailed into southern ports in the United States: Whites mistook the vessel for part of a war fleet set on liberating the slaves.

Cuffe operated many of his ships out of New Bedford, one of the leading centers of the whaling industry. The port's commerce was dominated by shrewd Quaker merchants, with whom Cuffe established strong business and social ties.

With the gains from the *Ranger*'s voyages, Cuffe invested in other businesses and properties. In 1799, he purchased a large new farm in Westport. Soon afterward, he bought a flour mill and a water-pumping windmill. These ventures provided work for his many relatives and helped establish the Cuffe family as a powerful commercial force in the Westport area. Cuffe's establishment of a public school in the late 1790s was yet another act that demonstrated his concern for the well-being of his family and the surrounding community.

By the turn of the century, the Cuffe and Wainer clan was the wealthiest business firm in Westport. Cuffe then looked beyond his ledger books and supply orders and began to think more and more about larger issues. Although his shipping business was thriving, he knew that his success was unusual and that the situation for most black Americans was bleak. He read grim reports of the atrocities that were committed against slaves in the South. He heard that some northern cities were placing restrictions on the number of blacks who could live in their communities. And he knew that some of the ships tied up next to the *Ranger*, when it was docked at New Bedford, Salem, and other northern ports, were heavily involved in the slave trade. He could not be satisfied with his own success while surrounded by these glaring examples of racial prejudice and oppression.

Cuffe's growing interest in the struggle for racial justice ultimately led him to the Quakers, the religious denomination of which his parents had been unofficial members. The Quakers, who were known for their humane and pacifist teachings, were the most influential of the organizations that were calling for an end to slavery, a cause known as abolitionism. They were strongly established in southern New England, where their penchant for hard work helped them to prosper as merchants and traders.

Many of Cuffe's friends and acquaintances within the shipping business were Quakers, and he was familiar with their way of life. The American branch of the Society of Friends had been established in the colonies in the 1600s by Quaker members who were fleeing religious persecution in England. The Quakers had a simple, distinctive way of dressing and spoke in a formal manner, using the words *thee* and *thou* in place of the word *you*. They had no official clergy and depended instead upon the inward light of God's word to guide them at prayer meetings. Their worship services, which were held in buildings known as meetinghouses, allowed for anyone in attendance to address the congregation.

The Quakers were strongly committed to helping blacks. The Society of Friends published numerous journals that denounced slavery, and its rule that no member could own slaves was a shining example to other religious denominations. In addition to helping slaves win their freedom, the Quakers were also involved in efforts to educate free blacks. In 1770, a Philadelphia Quaker named Anthony Benezet had

A page from the record book of a Philadelphia meetinghouse describes an inspirational dream that Cuffe related to the congregation. No matter whether he was working in Westport or traveling on business, he regularly attended meetings of the Society of Friends.

established a school for blacks, the first of many that the Quakers built.

Cuffe was attracted to the Quakers' principles and way of life, and he often attended their meetings in Westport or at other meetinghouses when he was traveling. He soon learned that he had a gift for speaking to others. During a service at the Arch Street Meeting House in Philadelphia, he told a group of young men about a vision he once had that had left a deep impression on him.

Cuffe recounted how a ghostly figure had appeared before him and asked what was troubling him. Cuffe answered the apparition that he did not know. The figure then told him the trouble was in his heart. It produced a sharp instrument that it used to separate Cuffe's heart from his body, and it held out the organ to him. The heart looked unclear and, related Cuffe, "contained all kinds of abominable things." Cuffe would never be healed, the figure said, until he submitted to having his heart cleansed.

Cuffe expressed hopelessness that he could be purified. Nevertheless, the ghostly figure asked him if he wanted to be cleansed, and Cuffe said yes. The figure then took the sharp instrument and, Cuffe said, "separated all that was vile and closed up the heart, replaced it, and healed the wound."

After telling this story, Cuffe looked at his entranced audience and asserted that the vision had made him a "changed man and new creature." He urged the young men to be similarly cleansed. He told them to find a "physician who could heal them," no matter how troubled their hearts might be.

Cuffe's ties with the Quakers also proved to be a boon to his shipping business. He established his first close trading association with James Brian, a Quaker merchant from Delaware. His business connections with William Rotch, Jr., who owned the largest shipping business in New England, were also useful in opening doors for him in other seaports.

In the early 1800s, the Society of Friends often held abolitionist meetings at the Arch Street Meeting House in Philadelphia. Cuffe, who had established a trading run between Westport and the City of Brotherly Love, was a frequent speaker there.

As Cuffe's business empire grew, he left the command of his ships to other captains while he made trading arrangements from his headquarters in Westport. In 1803, after building a larger ship for his fleet, the brig *Hero*, he began to expand his trade network across the Atlantic. The new ship sailed to France, Portugal, and Spain, while the *Ranger* continued to ply back and forth between New Bedford and Philadelphia. Cuffe was especially pleased when the *Hero* made its first voyage into African waters, during a whaling expedition in 1804.

In 1806, Cuffe returned to the helm of a ship to command the *Alpha*, the newly built giant of the Cuffe fleet. With his 14-year-old son Paul, Jr., aboard as a member of the crew, he sailed the *Alpha* to Savannah, Georgia. There he picked up a cargo of cotton that was to be delivered to a trading firm in the Russian port of St. Petersburg (now called Leningrad).

After sailing across the Atlantic, Cuffe docked the *Alpha* in the port of Göteborg, Sweden. The sight of the ship's all-black crew created a great amount of curiosity in the port and brought many visitors to the dockside. After a short time in Göteborg, Cuffe learned that the route to St. Petersburg was blocked by the opposing navies of France and Russia, which were then at war.

American travelers seeking to escape the hostilities flocked to the *Alpha* and booked their passage home. A Swedish boy named Abraham Rodin also boarded the ship and asked Cuffe if he could join its crew. Cuffe agreed, and with the American passengers and the young Swede on board, the *Alpha* soon sailed for America.

The return trip was not without its difficulties. The vessel nearly capsized during a horrendous storm off the coast of Greenland, and Cuffe was forced to dump much of his cargo to lighten the ship. The *Alpha* finally managed to dock at Philadelphia in September 1807, with Cuffe and his crew exhausted from their battles with the arctic gales.

Four months after Cuffe arrived home, the U.S. Congress put into effect the Enforcement Act of 1808, which banned the further importation of slaves into the United States. Cuffe and other abolitionists were cheered by the news, although they knew the law would be difficult to enforce. Indeed, far stronger measures would be needed to bring about an end to slavery in America.

In 1808, Cuffe took a large step toward involving himself in the national crusade against slavery when he formally joined the Society of Friends at a ceremony at the Westport meetinghouse. The Quakers' prayer meetings gave him the opportunity to speak out publicly on spiritual and political matters, and he did so with the enthusiasm of someone who has finally been given a voice after many years of silence. His addresses on Christian charity and the need to help the downtrodden black race were described by a fellow Quaker as being "short and moderately expressed but marked by good sense and a deep devotional feeling." Cuffe's words powerfully affected his audiences, which were mostly white, and during his travels he was often invited to lead the prayer services at various congregations.

Cuffe found much room for improvement in the way blacks were treated even in the Society of Friends. The Quakers, despite their Christian humility and their assertion that all men were equal, were no less prejudiced than other whites. Cuffe and other black Quakers had to sit on "Negro benches" in the back of the meetinghouse when they were attending services. This segregated seating arrangement was practiced as well by other religious denominations that accepted black members, prompting black Baptists, Methodists, and Episcopalians in a number of cities to break away from their white associates and form their own churches.

The United States banned the importation of slaves from Africa in 1808, the year after Cuffe completed his first voyage across the Atlantic. In this engraving, the U.S. frigate Constellation *chases a ship trying to smuggle slaves into a southern port.*

Philadelphia harbor around 1800. Cuffe's meetings with black leaders in Philadelphia and other cities convinced him that he should take a prominent role in the struggle against racial oppression. By 1808, he had become increasingly intrigued with the idea of starting a trade route to Africa and establishing a refuge there for blacks.

One day during a service in Philadelphia, Cuffe gave an especially moving sermon. Immediately afterward, the leader of the congregation invited Cuffe to sit beside him. Cuffe was surprised by this gesture and was touched that the congregation held him in such high esteem. But as he looked toward the back of the room, where the black members were sitting, he knew that he was not yet ready to sit with the whites. Thanking the Quaker elder for the invitation, he declined the offer and rejoined the other black members.

It was characteristic of Cuffe to keep his anger in check. He saw himself as a pioneer for other blacks who wanted to succeed in America, and he carefully cultivated his connections with influential white businessmen and clergymen. Among his closest white friends was the shipping tycoon William Rotch, Jr., who sometimes dined at Cuffe's house and who was glad to assist the black captain's business ventures.

Cuffe's success did not go unnoticed in America or abroad. Churches, antislavery organizations, and black social groups pointed to him as an example of what blacks could achieve if they were given the same rights and opportunities that whites had. British abolitionists were also impressed with what their American colleagues told them about the black shipowner. In 1807, the *Monthly Repository of Theology and General Literature*, a British journal that was also circulated in the United States, published an article on Cuffe's life entitled "Memoirs of an African Captain." The article stated that Cuffe had proved that "with equal advantages of education and circumstances, the Negro-race might fairly be compared with their white brethren on any part of the globe."

Cuffe had achieved a position of great prosperity by the time the article appeared. With the completion of his newest ship, the brig *Traveller*, in 1808, his fleet numbered four vessels and his trading connections stretched across the Atlantic. At the age of 49, he could look forward to quieter years ahead as he let his large squad of sons, nephews, and sons-in-law manage the family business.

But Cuffe was not ready to rest. America was not a land of freedom for his people, and he was not sure that he wanted to entrust the future of his children to his native country. Somewhere, he thought, there must be a place where blacks could live without having to feel the sting of the overseer's whip or to hear the taunts of bigots. Somewhere, his people would find the "land of milk and honey" that was described in the Bible.

As Cuffe searched the seas from the deck of the *Traveller*, he could see a faint glimmer of the promised land for which he was searching. His eyes were on Africa. ◖◗

PAUL

CAPTAIN

COFFEE

1812.

4
LAND OF FREEDOM

IN SEPTEMBER 1810, Cuffe presented an unusual proposal to the Westport Society of Friends: If they had, as he put it, "unity with his Prospect," he would voyage to West Africa and search for an area suitable for colonization by black American settlers. He knew the endeavor would require the assistance of numerous benefactors, and he especially wanted to enlist his fellow Quakers in the effort.

For nearly three years, Cuffe had been struggling with the questions surrounding the possibility of establishing a colony in Africa, and he had written to many people of influence seeking support for his venture. At one moment, he would sound a note of despair in his letters: "As to poor me, I feel very feeble and almost worn out in hard service and unable of doing much for my brethren the African race." But on the next page, he would continue more optimistically: "But blessed by God, I am what I am," and he vowed with stern Christian fortitude "ever to be submissive that His will may be done."

By 1810, Cuffe was sure that God was directing him to move to Africa. His commitment to African colonization stemmed from two ambitions: the desire to create a better home for America's free black population and the desire to end the slave trade in Africa. He well understood the obstacles in his way. For one thing, establishing a new colony in Africa would be very expensive and would require financial assistance. In addition, many Africans were heavily involved in

A silhouette illustration commemorating Cuffe's voyages. In 1809, he began preparing his newest ship, the Traveller, *for an expedition to Africa's west coast. "I am of the African race," he told his abolitionist friends in stating his intention of bringing the benefits of Christianity and Western civilization to the African natives.*

the slave trade and would need another means of support if the business was ended. Lastly, Cuffe would need the cooperation of the governments of Great Britain and the United States, a tricky business at a time when the two countries were embroiled in a heated dispute over trade regulations.

Cuffe had reached the conclusion that in order to end slavery in the United States, the illegal slave trade had to be stopped at its source, in Africa. He believed that the slave trade's hold on Africa could be broken by exposing the native population to the influence of Christianity and Western education. He could think of no better missionaries for the effort to "civilize" Africa than America's free blacks, whose skills and potential were largely being wasted in their own country. Moreover, the sea captain dreamed of forming a prosperous business community on the coast of West Africa; under the guidance of successful businessmen such as himself, this community would reach out to the people of Africa.

Cuffe had already spoken with a number of people about his interest in Africa by the autumn of 1810, when he presented his colonization idea to the Westport Quakers. Among those with whom he had consulted were Richard Allen, Absalom Jones, and James Forten—all leaders of Philadelphia's black community—and James Pemberton, the president of the Pennsylvania Abolition Society. But it was to the local branch of the Society of Friends that he made his first formal proposal about his African expedition.

Cuffe did not have a precise plan or timetable to present to the Westport Quakers. Instead, he gave a general sketch of his colonization proposal. He planned, he said, to sail to Africa to investigate the possibility of establishing a community that would foster a trading network between the United States, Europe, and Africa. This community would be the first step in the rebirth of the entire continent. Gradually, as the colony grew stronger and more prosperous, missionary groups would be sent inland to establish Christianity and trade. In the meantime, free black Americans would have a refuge from the racial persecution they suffered at home.

Cuffe's proposal met with nearly unanimous approval from the Westport Quakers. His friend William Rotch, Jr., pledged a large amount of financial support for the voyage, and the Society offered to provide him with formal letters of introduction to domestic and foreign philanthropic organizations. Leading abolitionists, including Dr. Benjamin Rush, also wrote letters of recommendation. Rush said in his letter: "I have had the pleasure of a personal

One of America's leading physicians, Dr. Benjamin Rush was also a staunch abolitionist. He assisted Cuffe's African venture by providing the black captain with a letter of recommendation to help him finance his voyage.

Little-Compton, July 4, 1809. (tf.)

Copartnership Formed.

THE Subscribers would inform their friends and the public, that they have lately commenced business under the firm of CUFF & HOWARDS— and have taken the Store lately occupied by RECORDS HEATH & SON, in *Water-street*, where they intend keeping a general assortment of

W. I. GOODS & GROCERIES ; and respectfully solicit a share of their custom.   PAUL CUFF.
            PETER HOWARD.
            ALEX. HOWARD.

They have now on hand—Fresh superfine Alexandria Flour, Rice, Philad. Pilot Bread and Biscuit ; loaf, Havana and brown Sugars ; Hyson, Souchong, and Bohea Teas, Coffee, Chocolate, Pearlash, Ginger, Allspice, Pepper, Cinnamon, Cloves, Nutmegs, Honey, Vinegar, Allum, Sulphur and roll Brimstone, Copperas, Logwood, Redwood, Spanish Flotant Indigo, Flax, Sole and upper Leather, Calf-Skins and Sheep Legs, an assortment of Philadelphia Earthen Ware, and a variety of other articles.

New-Bedford, 7th mo. 0, 1809.

Cuffe prepared for his initial voyage to Africa during a time when he had a financial stake in many enterprises, including the business announced in this flyer: a household goods and grocery store in New Bedford that was managed by his sons-in-law Peter and Alexander Howard.

knowledge of Capt. Paul Cuffe for several years and from his conduct and conversation, as well as from the character I have uniformly heard of him from all who know him, I have been led to entertain a high opinion of his integrity and other moral virtues. . . . He is hereby recommended to the notice and protection of the friends of liberty, humanity and religion in every part of the world."

Excited by the mounting support for his African colonization plan, Cuffe immediately set to work to organize his initial reconnaissance voyage. He hoped that his own resources would enable him to pay for much of the expedition's expenses. After all, a household goods trading venture that he had recently formed with two of his sons-in-law, Alexander and Peter Howard, was prospering. In addition, Cuffe planned to sail to Africa with a cargo that he expected would cover the cost of the expedition. But the purpose of the voyage was not to search for profit but rather to scout the possibilities.

Cuffe's destination, the British West African colony of Sierra Leone, was an area marked by an often tragic history. Founded in one of the chief centers of the slave trade, the colony had barely survived the effects of floods, disease, and starvation during its 34-year existence. Cuffe was well aware of the drawbacks of the region, but with only limited resources of his own, he had little choice but to sail to the colony that had already been established as a refuge for free blacks. Moreover, even though the colony was British, it had a long connection to America's former slaves.

The history of Sierra Leone had begun shortly after the end of the American Revolution in 1783. At that time, Britain had in her domain several thousand American slaves who had escaped from the colonies with the departing British troops. Some of these blacks were resettled in Canada, but the majority

In the 1780s, the slums of London became home to large numbers of former slaves who had aided the British during the American Revolution. But before long, philanthropic organizations began resettling these destitute blacks in a colony in Africa.

were taken back to England, where the impoverished refugees congregated in a decrepit slum area of London.

In 1786, a group of London businessmen formed the Committee for the Black Poor, an organization devoted to assisting the former slaves. The committee was extremely interested when Henry Smeathman, an amateur botanist who had lived for many years in West Africa, proposed resettling the destitute population on the African coast. The Flycatcher, as Smeathman called himself, assured the businessmen that there were great commercial opportunities in Africa for those who invested in the colony.

Although Smeathman's proposal was adopted by the British government, he died before the expedition could be organized. The Flycatcher's position as leader of the African colonization movement was then assumed by Granville Sharp, a noted social re-former and supporter of black rights. Sharp's concern for London's black population was based on human-itarian concerns. Yet the history of Sierra Leone was to be marred from the start by the actions of profit-minded merchants who supplied the colony.

On April 8, 1787, nearly 350 black immigrants, accompanied by about 100 white settlers who were drawn to Africa by the promise of free land, departed England for Sierra Leone. The passenger total would have been larger, but many blacks had turned away from the colonization effort for fear that they would be sent to a prison community.

Granville Sharp talks with a sick man at his office in London. The British philanthropist organized the first attempt to establish a colony at Sierra Leone on the coast of West Africa. The Province of Freedom—Sharp's name for his haven for England's black poor—failed as a colony, however, and the outpost had to be taken over by a London-based company.

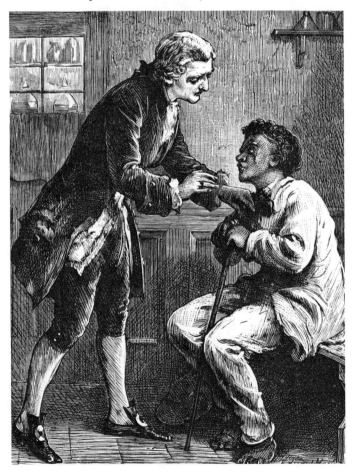

The original colony, which Sharp named the Province of Freedom because it was a self-governing, democratic community, was doomed from the start. Malaria and other diseases ravaged the settlers, and many deserted the colony to live with the natives. Started with the best of intentions, the colony was taken over by the Sierra Leone Company, a sympathetic British trading firm, in 1791. In 1807, the nearly bankrupt company passed the reins back to the British government.

The directors of the defunct Sierra Leone Company were for the most part philanthropists and clergymen. This group—including such prominent British politicians and abolitionists as William Wilberforce, Zachary Macaulay, and William Allen—then formed the African Institution, an organization devoted to the welfare of the Sierra Leone colonists. By late 1810, when Cuffe was preparing to set out for the colony, Sierra Leone had gained a toehold on the African continent, and numerous villages ringed the capital of Freetown.

Cuffe had been interested in traveling to Sierra Leone ever since he had first heard of the colony. He wrote, "Having been informed that there was a settlement of people of colour at Sierra Leone under the immediate guardianship of a civilized power, I have for these many years past felt a lively interest in their behalf." His plans to establish a whaling company and a center of industry and commerce in Africa excited the members of the African Institution, including Zachary Macaulay, a former governor of Sierra Leone. Writing that "a person like Paul Cuffe would most unquestionably be a desirable accession to the population of Sierra Leone," the British philanthropist invited Cuffe to the colony.

·Armed with invitations and letters of recommendation, Cuffe raised the *Traveller*'s sails and departed from Westport on November 25, 1810. The Cuffe

family and the local Quakers gathered at the dockside to give him and his crew a rousing send-off. His crew included three of his nephews: Thomas Wainer, John Wainer, and Michael Wainer, Jr. Also on board were seven black men from Westport: John Marsters, Samuel Hicks, Zachariah White, Joseph Hemnaway, Charles Freeberg, Prince Edwards, and Thomas Paton.

Stopping first in Philadelphia, Cuffe delivered a load of barley and organized a meeting with the Philadelphia Quaker community so that he could discuss his upcoming voyage. Word of Cuffe's expedition had spread throughout the city, and a large crowd gath-

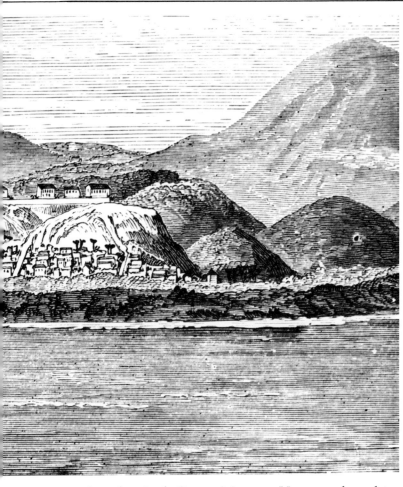

In December 1810, Cuffe steered the Traveller *toward Sierra Leone. Accompanying him was a crew of nine men, "all people of color," he stated proudly.*

ered at the Arch Street Meeting House to hear him speak. He was a little uneasy about the meeting because he had heard that some people were saying his real reason for traveling to Sierra Leone was to find a profitable new market for his shipping business. The meeting went well, however, and Cuffe was given the blessings of the Quakers and the black community.

The spiritual welfare of his people rather than the desire for profit was what motivated Cuffe to sail to Sierra Leone, as was attested to by John James, a Philadelphia Quaker merchant and abolitionist with whom the black captain had done much trading.

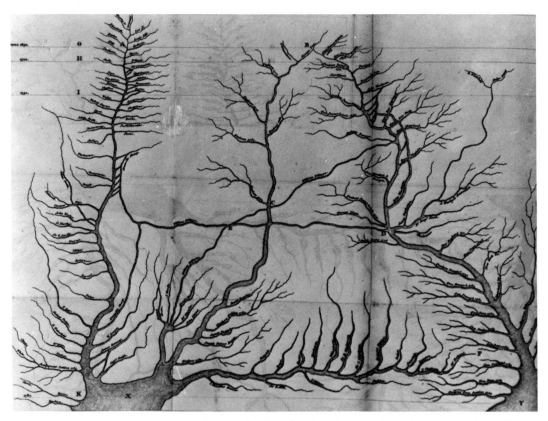

A map from Thomas Clarkson's book, The History of the Rise, Progress and Accomplishment of the Abolition of the African Slave Trade, *shows river routes used by slave traders in West Africa. Cuffe read the book during his voyage to Sierra Leone.*

James had a load of corn that he wanted Cuffe to take to Portugal. Cuffe already had a small cargo of general goods that he planned to trade in Sierra Leone to cover the cost of the journey. Although the opportunity for profit must have been tempting to him, he turned down the cargo, telling James that he would not make any detour on his passage to Africa. In the journal he kept of his voyage, he stated, "It was not for the profit of grain [sales] that I had undertaken this voyage."

On December 27, 1810, Cuffe and his men waved good-bye to a crowd on the docks of Philadelphia and set sail for Africa. Proud of the mission on which they were engaged, the *Traveller's* crew looked forward excitedly to the voyage as their ship began to plow its way across the Atlantic.

The first few weeks of the trip were uneventful, and on the rainy but windless night of January 20, 1811, Cuffe wrote that his crew was confident God was smiling on their voyage. "Our minds was collected together to wait on the Lord," he recorded, "not withstanding we were on the great deep."

But on the last day of January, a storm struck, and the *Traveller* was buffeted by gale-force winds and drenched by giant waves that washed over its decks. One of the waves swept up John Marsters and carried him overboard. For a moment, Cuffe thought the crewman was lost, but Marsters grabbed hold of some loose rigging that was dangling from the side of the ship and pulled himself back on board.

Was the storm an omen of difficult times ahead? However unnerved Cuffe might have been by the storm and the near death of one of his crew members, he recorded only that in the following days there were gentle breezes and "clear weather and pleasant smooth seas" as they continued on to Africa.

For the remainder of the voyage, Cuffe spent much time reading *The History of the Rise, Progress and Accomplishment of the Abolition of the African Slave Trade*, a book by an English abolitionist named Thomas Clarkson. The book led Cuffe to new insights into the causes of slavery and helped him understand what further efforts were needed to bring about a complete end to the slave trade in Africa.

After three weeks at sea, the *Traveller* had sailed halfway across the Atlantic; Cuffe was drawing ever closer to his arrival at the land of his dreams. Finally, the westerly winds that had carried him steadily toward Africa began to change and blow from the east. On February 21, 1811, he wrote in his journal, "The dust of Africa lodged on our rigging."

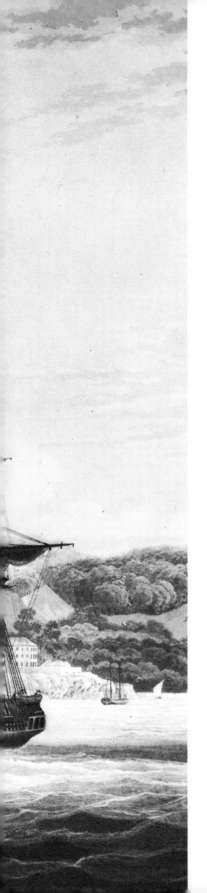

5

THE NATIONS
OF AFRICA

NEARLY MOTIONLESS BECAUSE of the absence of wind, the *Traveller* slipped into African coastal waters on February 24, 1811. On their first day there, the crew enjoyed a bounty from the rich fishing areas near the African shore. "Caught one dolphin and many suckerfish," Cuffe wrote. "So we had an excellent fish dinner for the first time since we sailed from America." Continuing down the coast of North Africa, Cuffe and his shipmates soon caught sight of the mountains of Sierra Leone. On March 1, the ship dropped anchor in the harbor of Freetown.

The Portuguese mariners who had explored this area in the 15th century had named it Sierra Leone, the Mountains of the Lion, after the steep, green mountains that dominated the coastline. The peaks formed a backdrop against which the small Freetown community lay. The town was fronted by a spacious harbor that was wide and deep enough for large ships, which fit well with Cuffe's plans to use the harbor as a base of trading operations.

As Cuffe gazed around the harbor, he spotted a small schooner of the type that was used in local, small-scale trading. But there were other vessels in the harbor that were used for more sinister purposes.

On March 1, 1811, Cuffe and his crew docked the Traveller *in Freetown harbor beneath the imposing mountains of Sierra Leone.*

From their shape, he recognized the vessels to be slave ships, and he guessed that they had been captured by the British frigate that was also docked in the harbor. The slave ships were a dispiriting sight for Cuffe on his first day in the beautiful and serene harbor.

The thickly forested coast of Sierra Leone had a long connection with the slave trade, from its first Portuguese occupiers to its later British rulers. Although Great Britain had abolished the trade in African slaves within all parts of its empire in 1807, illegal trading was still common. The British navy captured some of the slavers, but the majority escaped detection. When slavers were arrested, their captive cargoes were set free, often in Sierra Leone. Cuffe discovered when he arrived at Freetown that there were more than a thousand of these former captives, known as liberated slaves, living in poverty and hunger in groups of huts ringing the town. Few of them knew any English or were familiar with Western agricultural methods, and their presence imposed a huge burden on the colony.

Cuffe was eager to tour Sierra Leone and speak with the settlers, but his first task was to arrange for the sale of his ship's cargo. From the reports of other American traders who had visited the colony, he knew that he might have some trouble conducting business in Freetown. American traders had to pay high import duties on the goods they sold, and sometimes they were forbidden by British government officials from doing any business in the port.

On his second day in Freetown, the American captain received his first taste of the difficulties to come. As he was about to begin an exploration of Freetown with his crew, Sierra Leone's governor, Edward Henry Columbine, approached the ship and demanded that he be allowed to come aboard. After walking up and down the deck and reading through the cargo inventory, the governor ordered that six bales of Cuffe's American cloth goods be prohibited from sale, as well as some grain and meat.

Aghast at the harsh decision, Cuffe explained to Columbine the purpose of his visit to Sierra Leone and produced letters of introduction from British abolitionist leaders. After brooding for a while, the governor relented and gave him permission to sell the foodstuffs and other perishable items in his cargo. Relieved, Cuffe offered Columbine some food and drink and in return received an invitation to dine at the governor's residence.

Cuffe discovered at his dinner with the governor that Columbine was a dispirited and frustrated man.

Cuffe saw clear evidence of the presence of slave traders as soon as he arrived in Freetown. Moored around the harbor were the hulks of a half dozen slave ships that had been captured by the British navy.

A church and school at a village near Freetown. Cuffe was impressed with the strides that Sierra Leone's settlers had made to establish an educational system and to bring Christianity to the local African tribes.

He had been governor of Sierra Leone for less than two years, but already he had lost his wife to malaria and had been forced to send his children home to England to protect their health. He relied heavily on his fellow white administrative officials and merchants who controlled the colony's daily affairs, and though somewhat sympathetic to the needs of the colony's black settlers, he complained that many of them were beggars or smugglers. He was interested in Cuffe's plans for developing African industries and commerce but could do little to assist the black captain.

Cuffe was not discouraged by Columbine's picture of Sierra Leone as a disease-ridden, backwater colony riddled with corruption and racial conflict. The same reports had circulated in the United States, and Cuffe had come to Sierra Leone knowing he would encounter problems. Now that he was there, standing on the streets of Freetown, he decided to see if he could build his African trading network.

At first, Cuffe's attempts to sell his cargo in Freetown did not go well. British traders, eager to maintain the exploitative monopoly they held over the colony's commerce, were determined to thwart the black captain and send him home in discouragement. When Cuffe presented his goods for sale, the Freetown merchants offered him extremely low prices. He began to fear that his trip to Africa might become a huge financial loss.

Cuffe decided he must turn elsewhere to find fair business dealings. Suspecting that he might have better luck speaking with Freetown's black tradesmen, he began to explore the town and meet with its residents. On his first trip, he was especially drawn to places of learning. "Visited the school of 30 girl scholars," he wrote in his journal, "which was a pleasing prospect in Sierra Leone." There were two girls' schools in Freetown, which offered courses in needlework, reading, writing, and arithmetic. This, Cuffe decided, was a definite sign of black progress.

From his visits with the citizens of Freetown, Cuffe learned what he could about the history of black immigration to the colony. Two of the men he met, the carpenters Peter Francis and David Edmonds, were members of a group of American slaves who had escaped from their masters and taken refuge in the Canadian province of Nova Scotia after the American Revolution. During the 1790s, many of the black Nova Scotians had been enticed to Sierra Leone by the promise of free land, and they had quickly established themselves as industrious members of the community. Trouble arose later, however, when colonial officials tried to charge them rent for their land. The angry settlers rebelled, but they were defeated by British troops, and many were expelled from the colony. Those remaining were still viewed as troublemakers by Sierra Leone's administrators.

Cuffe also met with John Leedham Morgan, who had held a number of government posts in the colony. Morgan was a Jamaican-born Maroon, a descendant of a group of fierce rebel slaves who had won their freedom from their British rulers on the West Indian island. In 1800, more than 400 Maroon farmers had accepted a British offer to move them to Sierra Leone, but the settlers had not been particularly successful in working the colony's poor soil.

Both the Nova Scotians and the Maroons were interested in Cuffe's business ideas, and they introduced him to local tribesmen with whom they traded. He established trade dealings with members of the Kru tribe, a coastal people who were numerous in the villages around Freetown. Famed for their skill as sailors, the Kru were also involved in many types of trade. Cuffe hired a number of the Kru to help him dispose of his cargo and to acquire lumber from inland areas.

Cuffe had not been in Freetown long when he was notified that he would be receiving a visit from African royalty. King Thomas, a local tribal ruler, appeared soon afterward at the side of the *Traveller* with a retinue of warriors. The meeting between the black captain, who was eager to discuss his antislavery views and Quaker beliefs, and the elderly chieftain, who was curious about Cuffe's trade ideas, was a great success for Cuffe. He wrote excitedly in his journal that King Thomas "appeared to be sober and grave. I treated him with civility and made him a present of a bible, a history of slavery . . . accompanied with a letter of advice from myself such as appeared to me to be good to hand to the king for the use and encouragement of the nations of Africa."

Clearly, Cuffe made a favorable impression upon the king, who put in a good word for him with other

tribal chieftains. A short time later, Cuffe was invited to visit King George, the ruler of the nearby coastal region of Bullom. Accompanied by a group of settlers, Cuffe made the trip to King George's village, and the king, Cuffe recorded, "received and treated us very cordially." The king was pleased with the Bible and religious pamphlets he received from his visitor, and Cuffe was equally delighted with the three chickens he received from his host.

At the end of March, Cuffe met a group of Mandingo, who were members of a tribe that followed the Islamic faith. Cuffe was impressed with the deep religious convictions of this tribe, but he was troubled by their attitude toward slavery. Still active in the business of capturing and selling slaves, the Mandingo did not want to see the trade completely abolished.

Settlers arrive at Sierra Leone in 1787. Unable to negotiate fair prices for the Traveller's cargo with the colony's white British businessmen, Cuffe sold his merchandise through Freetown's black tradesmen. Before he left the colony, he helped organize a black trade association called the Friendly Society.

A group of African traders travel through a palm forest in Sierra Leone. Among the goods that Cuffe bought from Freetown merchants and native traders were palm oil, ivory, exotic woods, and animal hides.

When Cuffe challenged them about their slave dealings and urged them to turn to Christianity, they responded with a fierce affirmation of pride in their African heritage and Islamic beliefs.

Slave trading continued to plague the African coasts, but a visit to Freetown's courthouse helped to bolster Cuffe's confidence that the colony was doing what it could to halt the practice. He witnessed a Portuguese captain being convicted for slave dealing. The guilty man's ship was impounded for use in returning his captives to their homes. Cuffe knew that the conviction of one slaver would not stop the trade, but he hoped that the fear of being captured by British warships would make most slave traders decide that the business was too risky.

Despite Cuffe's strong interest in ending slavery, his main priority in coming to Africa was to help build a base of black industry there. By working closely with Freetown's black businessmen, he was able to sell his ship's cargo and purchase new merchandise for his return voyage. Among these business associates, Cuffe found men who were willing to risk the anger of Freetown's officials by supporting his plans for reforming the colony's restrictive trading regulations.

By early April, the *Traveller* was ready to sail, but Cuffe was not yet finished with his work in Sierra Leone. Enlisting the support of a group of black tradesmen and merchants, he drew up a petition calling for the British government to support black American immigration to Sierra Leone and to give foreign traders the right to expand their commercial ties in the colony. Cuffe's pointed reference to the establishing of a local whaling industry, a business that he was hoping to plunge into, was all part of his plan for developing the commercial power of the colony's black community.

The response to the petition among Freetown's black population was enthusiastic. A group of settlers immediately formed the Friendly Society, a mutual-aid organization that was founded to promote the business interests of the black community.

Cuffe's excitement over the developments in Sierra Leone increased after he received a letter from William Allen, the African Institution administrator, in mid-April. The Londoner wrote that the British government, at the urging of his organization, had voted to allow Cuffe to apply for special permits to trade between England and Sierra Leone. Allen urged Cuffe to come to England immediately so that he

A captive stands chained to a pole at an African slave depot. Some tribes in West Africa sold war captives to white slavers, and they resented the attempts by Sierra Leone's settlers and colonial administration to bring an end to the trade.

could meet with the leaders of the African Institution and get his trading licenses approved.

In the meantime, unbeknownst to Cuffe, a Sierra Leone official, Judge Alexander Smith, was doing his best to destroy the American captain's reputation among the members of the African Institution. Angered by Cuffe's attempt to break the British traders' hold on the colony's economy, Smith wrote a scathing denunciation of Cuffe to African Institution official Zachary Macaulay, saying that "he had never known a more mercenary or unprincipled man, except perhaps a slavetrader."

Smith's letter indicated the bitterness that Cuffe's activities aroused among Sierra Leone's white merchants. The members of the African Institution did not believe Smith's charges. But the letter later caused Cuffe some embarrassment.

Cuffe sailed from Freetown in May 1811, after spending two months surveying conditions in Sierra Leone. His destination was England, where he hoped to find support for his idea of building a vigorous three-way trade network between Africa, Europe, and America.

Two months after arriving in Freetown, Cuffe decided that he had finished the tasks he had set for himself on his first exploratory mission to Sierra Leone. He had scouted commercial markets, nailed down business connections, and won official approval to trade in the colony. Now he must move forward and establish the trading network that would tie together the peoples and nations of Africa. His first matter of business was to meet with Allen, Macaulay, and his other allies in London.

Cuffe and most of his crew made final preparations for the voyage to England. Thomas Wainer, Cuffe's nephew, chose to remain in Freetown. One new crew member, a young colonist named Aaron Richards, signed on as an apprentice. On May 10, 1811, the *Traveller* left Sierra Leone's peaks behind and set sail for the north. ❧

6

TO ENGLAND
AND BACK

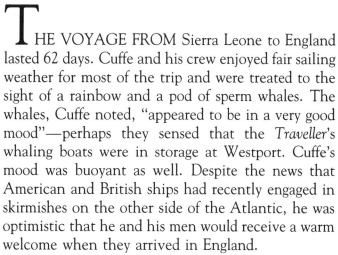

THE VOYAGE FROM Sierra Leone to England lasted 62 days. Cuffe and his crew enjoyed fair sailing weather for most of the trip and were treated to the sight of a rainbow and a pod of sperm whales. The whales, Cuffe noted, "appeared to be in a very good mood"—perhaps they sensed that the *Traveller*'s whaling boats were in storage at Westport. Cuffe's mood was buoyant as well. Despite the news that American and British ships had recently engaged in skirmishes on the other side of the Atlantic, he was optimistic that he and his men would receive a warm welcome when they arrived in England.

But Cuffe and his crew were not so fortunate. Soon after the *Traveller* docked in Liverpool, a huge port on the west coast of England, two crew members left the ship and went exploring. They never returned.

Cuffe soon learned that the two men had been seized by a press-gang—a terror of English harbor towns. Press-gangs were groups of ruffians from the dockside areas that roamed the streets in search of seamen whom they could kidnap. Great Britain was at war with France at the time, and the Royal Navy

London was both a bustling commercial center and the capital of the largest empire in the world when Cuffe visited the city in 1811. His quest for support for his African trading venture brought him into contact with the British nobility and some of the leading members of Parliament.

Shortly after the Traveller *docked in Liverpool, three of the ship's crew members were seized by press-gangs for the British navy. Cuffe's struggle to get his men released received national attention in Britain's newspapers.*

was glad to pay a bounty to anyone who could bring candidates to the naval recruiting offices. Impressment, the seizing of able-bodied men for the navy, was a perfectly legal maneuver.

Cuffe had no intention of letting any of his crew be impressed into the British navy. He immediately confronted the leaders of the press-gang and demanded the release of his crew members on the grounds that they were American citizens. His argument persuaded the leaders of the press-gang to set the two men free.

The battle with press-gangs had just begun, however. While Cuffe was liberating his two crew members, a different press-gang climbed aboard the *Traveller* and took away Aaron Richards, the Sierra Leonean apprentice. Claiming Richards as a British subject, the press-gang refused to let him go and sold him to the navy. Frustrated, Cuffe wrote: "I attended to getting Aaron his liberty. Used every influence as I was capable of, but all in vain. I then interceded with my friends, but in vain."

Cuffe's friends in Liverpool—a group of sympathetic merchants, abolitionists, and Quakers—tried to help win Richards's release. But days passed and they made no progress. Meanwhile, the British press took notice of Cuffe and created quite a stir about the black sea captain and his all-black crew. Although pleased to be a center of publicity, Cuffe was more concerned about the welfare of his impressed sailor.

Cuffe had appointments to keep with members of the African Institution in London, so he took a stagecoach to the city. There he encountered a newspaper reporter who later described him as being of "an agreeable countenance . . . he is both tall and stout, speaks English well, dresses in the Quaker style, in a drab-coloured suit, and wears a large flapped white hat."

Cuffe immediately set about meeting the men with whom he had corresponded for more than three years. His first two conferences were with the Quaker scientist and social reformer William Allen and the abolitionist politician William Wilberforce. Both men promised to use their influence in trying to free Aaron Richards, and they listened with interest as Cuffe discussed his ideas for founding indigenous business and trade industries in Africa.

While in London, Cuffe met with many government officials and prominent citizens and was successful in enlisting support for his plans for Sierra Leone. He was especially pleased to meet Thomas Clarkson, whose book on the abolition of the slave trade had impressed him during his voyage to Africa. Clarkson also took up Richards's cause, and he and Allen were at last successful in persuading the navy to release Richards. Cuffe expressed his relief in a typically understated manner in his journal upon hearing the good news: "You may think that was great consolation to me to think God permitted that I should have the happy opportunity of returning Aaron to his parents and fellow citizens of Sierra Leone."

With Richards safely back on board the *Traveller*, Cuffe once more devoted his full attention to his plans for Africa. The many distinguished letters of recommendation he carried opened doors for him. Nevertheless, it was his moving descriptions of the plight of the African people that impressed those with whom he talked. Among the people who listened attentively to Cuffe were Zachary Macaulay, the philanthropist and colonial administrator; Stephen Grillet, the noted French-American Quaker preacher; William and Richard Rathbone, both abolitionists and humanitarians; William Roscoe, a member of Parliament who organized Liverpool antislavery societies; and John Fussel, another member of Parlia-

William Allen was one of the directors of the African Institution, an organization that provided financial assistance to the settlers in Sierra Leone. Cuffe met with the organization's members several times to discuss commercial ventures, he said, "whereby Africa might be advantaged."

ment and a social reformer. They were all men of influence in British society, and Cuffe needed their assistance in getting permits to trade with Sierra Leone free of interference from rival merchants.

During his stay in London, Cuffe found William Allen to be especially supportive of his African venture. They often discussed the subject of African colonization until late in the evening, sharing their ideas about how the colony at Sierra Leone could be improved. Cuffe stated that he wanted a strong trade channel opened between America and Africa and also proposed that black American colonists be welcomed to Sierra Leone. Allen, enthusiastic about the American shipowner's plans, vowed to help him overcome British resistance to American intervention in the colony. Allen was impressed by Cuffe's intelligence and energy and described the captain in his diary with the words: "He seems like a man made on purpose for business; he has great experience as well as integrity."

Not all of Cuffe's time was spent on business matters; he also managed to take in the sights of London. Among the places he visited were the Tower of London, the houses of Parliament, St. Paul's Cathedral, and the London Bridge. He took a special interest in the national mint and made precise notes about the new steam engines that were being used there to produce coins at an astoundingly fast rate.

After spending a few weeks in London, Cuffe returned to Liverpool to arrange cargoes for the *Traveller* and the *Alpha*, which was also in port at that time. On the trip back to the England's west coast, he stopped in the town of Tedbury, where he was told about a woman who had lived there for many years until her death two weeks before. She was reported to have lived for more than three years without eating, drinking, or sleeping. "This appears to be a very singular circumstance," Cuffe wrote, "and must

be the power of the Almighty Director." He hoped that such favor would also be cast on his African venture.

A few days after Cuffe returned to Liverpool, he received a letter from William Allen informing him that the trading permits he was seeking would be arriving shortly. Cuffe continued with his business preparations and also attended many church meetings, at which he spoke out about the need for more Christian missions in Africa. Not everyone shared his enthusiasm for Africa, however; he had to say a sad farewell to crew member John Marsters, who had asked to return to America.

In late August, after Cuffe received the trading licenses and permits he had been seeking, he was told

Cuffe witnessed some of the latest advances of the 19th-century Industrial Revolution on a visit to the British national mint in London. At that time, new steam-powered presses were being used to replace manual-labor methods of stamping coins.

that the directors of the African Institution wanted to hold a meeting to hear about his African plans. He rushed back to London for the meeting, which was presided over by the Duke of Gloucester, King George III's brother. As a featured speaker, Cuffe discussed the living conditions in Sierra Leone and proposed steps that could be taken to spur business and trade in the region. He talked at length about the artistic achievements of the African people and presented the Duke of Gloucester with an African robe, letter box, and dagger. The objects proved, he said, "that the African was capable of mental endowments." The committee members, as Cuffe anticipated, fully endorsed his plans for building up the African economy.

After the meeting, Cuffe left London for the last time. On the way to Liverpool, he visited Manchester to see the city's cotton factories, which were the showcases of the Industrial Revolution, a melding of new steam-engine technology and commercial entrepreneurship that was transforming the English economy. Cuffe toured the Manchester factories and responded with the enthusiasm he had felt earlier, in the presence of the steam engines at the national mint. The new technology seemed a wonder to him, and the work—quick, efficient, and clean—seemed more dignified to Cuffe than manual labor. Marveling

Cuffe was highly impressed with the tremendous industrial capacity of the cotton factories in Manchester, England. After his visit to the city, he began to consider the possibility of building similar manufacturing centers in Africa.

at the speed of the new cotton-spinning machines, he wrote, "They have got them to perfection."

Intrigued by the possibility of bringing the industrial age to Africa, Cuffe returned to Liverpool and completed the arrangements for his return voyage to Sierra Leone. Accompanying him and his crew were four missionaries who were being sent by English Methodist churches to educate the natives and spread the influence of Christianity. On September 10, 1811, with Bibles and bales of cloth safely packed away in the *Traveller*'s storage hold, the ship weighed anchor and sailed from the port. Cuffe left England with a satisfied feeling, knowing that he now possessed the permits he needed to continue his efforts to establish a home for black Americans in Africa.

Once at sea, Cuffe searched the sky and water for a sign of what lay ahead. The first omen seemed bad. A French warship, observing the *Traveller* sailing from an English harbor, chased the ship and nearly captured it.

Then stormy seas battered Cuffe's ship. He noted during calmer days that sharks were pursuing the vessel and, he wrote, "seemed to be very fierce and ravenous." As the ship entered the tropics, the African heat began to blanket the ship. Men became short-tempered, and fights broke out. Cuffe was hard-pressed to maintain order.

Cuffe and his crew were relieved when their ship finally arrived in Freetown harbor and they could again set their feet on land. But the storms and fights were not yet behind them. Cuffe had an inkling that there would be difficulties ahead when he tried to unload his cargo and found himself blocked by an order from Charles Maxwell, the new governor of Sierra Leone. Maxwell stalled for a few days while studying Cuffe's trading permits but finally allowed the cargo to be unloaded under strict supervision. Cuffe noted with mild disdain, "I have an officer put

A page from Cuffe's journal, recorded on his voyage from Liverpool to Freetown in late 1811. During his second visit to Sierra Leone, the American captain traveled throughout the colony in search of places where he could plant the seeds of black industry.

on board my vessel to see the cargo landed, it being the first vessel that ever had been so waited upon in this port."

As soon as the *Traveller's* cargo was safely on shore, Cuffe began selling his goods, trying as much as possible to deal with Freetown's black merchants. He also directed his efforts toward expanding the Friendly Society, the trading organization that he had helped form during his previous visit. Now, with the sponsorship of the colony's Methodist congregations, the Friendly Society of Sierra Leone worked to promote economic cooperation within the black community.

Cuffe hoped that the Friendly Society would be the first of many cooperative organizations that would be started in Africa to promote international trade. Once the organization became strong enough to participate fully in his planned three-way trade network with America and Europe, the process of rooting out the slave trade in Africa could be waged effectively. An African economy that developed natural resources and native crafts for the world market, and an African export market that was directed by native leadership with cooperation from the Western countries—these were all part of Cuffe's dream.

In London, the African Institution was working to make Cuffe's dream come true. The organization's directors had succeeded in getting the government to set up new trade regulations for Sierra Leone that allowed the colony's exported goods to be sold at rates favorable to Freetown's merchants. William Allen and a group of his associates also donated a large sum of money to the Friendly Society of Sierra Leone to fund its expansion. Encouraged by the support of his friends in London, Cuffe became even more enthusiastic about the future of the colony and the prospects of developing the native economy.

But the three months that Cuffe spent in Sierra Leone during his second visit to the colony were not

without problems. A flu epidemic swept through Freetown, leaving his crew members Samuel Hicks and
Thomas Wainer seriously ill; although Hicks quickly
regained his health, Wainer's illness lingered for more
than a month. In addition, Cuffe became engaged in
a running business dispute with Judge Alexander
Smith, the white merchant who had previously written an abusive letter about Cuffe to the African Institution. Smith was determined to upset the
American captain's plans for encouraging black commercial activity and did everything he could to harass
Cuffe. The irascible and unscrupulous merchant con-
tracted for part of Cuffe's tobacco shipment, but then
refused to pay the agreed price for the goods, falsely
claiming that they were of bad quality.

The months at Sierra Leone were difficult for
Cuffe for other reasons, as well. Governor Maxwell's
new colonial administration imposed additional taxes
and civil restrictions on the settler population, which
sparked angry protests from the black community.
Cuffe was caught in the middle, for he sympathized
with the settlers but was afraid to do anything that
would cause him to lose the goodwill of the British
government. In fact, his association with the Friendly
Society, an organization that Governor Maxwell
viewed with suspicion, resulted in his being kept
under special watch by the colonial administration.

The cautious sea captain tried to keep a low profile
while he continued his search for new business opportunities in the colony. On a visit to a bay a short
distance from Freetown, he found a location that he
believed would be perfect for a timber-processing
mill. He also investigated areas in the nearby hills
that he thought might be suitable for cotton and
coffee cultivation. Thinking back to his visit to the
Manchester cotton factories, he began to imagine
what effect the founding of industries in the area
would have on the native population. By the end of
his stay in Sierra Leone in early 1812, he had come

A Methodist church in Sierra Leone, built in 1812. Unlike the enclave of white merchants at Freetown, the colony's missionaries generally supported the efforts of Cuffe and his associates in the Friendly Society to develop opportunities for black businessmen.

up with a number of ideas about how to turn Freetown into a thriving port.

As Cuffe prepared to leave Freetown and return to the United States, he became caught up in a number of different concerns. Samuel Hicks and Prince Edwards were set on staying in Sierra Leone, and Cuffe needed to find replacements for them. He was pleased when four colonists joined his crew—a sign, to Cuffe, of a coming wave of seafaring Africans. Another matter that Cuffe attended to was patching up his quarrel with Alexander Smith. In a final compromise with Smith, he accepted a load of wood as payment for his previously delivered tobacco shipment. Cuffe, relieved to have Smith at least temporarily off his back, wrote that "when men are like lions, we must be careful how we get our hands in their mouths."

Cuffe's departure from Sierra Leone was a sad event for the settler community, especially his associates in the Friendly Society. The colonists had begun to see him as a man who could bring about revolutionary change in their society and help them take control of their future. Although Cuffe was also sorry to leave the colony, he knew he had to return home so that he could begin work on his plan to transport black Americans to Africa. As a parting message to the colonists, he advised them, in true Quaker fashion, to serve as good examples to others, "doing justly, loving mercy, and walking humbly."

On the morning of February 11, 1812, the *Traveller* pulled up anchor and sailed from Freetown. But Cuffe did not get very far from Sierra Leone. His ship was stopped a short way out to sea by a British warship and taken back to port. His Sierra Leonean crew members, British officials claimed, were not supposed to be on his ship.

Cuffe and his crew were forced to wait in Freetown for eight more days before Governor Maxwell issued an apology to him, stating that the captain of the British ship had simply made an error. Cuffe graciously accepted the apology and once again took his ship out to sea. After almost a year in Africa and England, he was eager to return home. ✿

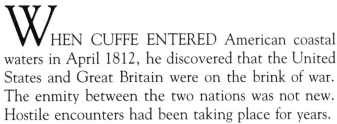

7

THE LONG
WAIT

WHEN CUFFE ENTERED American coastal waters in April 1812, he discovered that the United States and Great Britain were on the brink of war. The enmity between the two nations was not new. Hostile encounters had been taking place for years.

In 1807, the American warship *Chesapeake* had been fired upon and seized by a British warship, which removed four alleged British deserters from the American ship. Tensions continued to grow during the next five years as British ships enforced a tight naval blockade of France, with which Britain was at war. The British turned away the trading vessels of neutral countries from French ports, an interference that infuriated the Americans. The United States finally declared war on Great Britain on June 18, 1812.

Cuffe was worried that his plans for an African trade route would be jeopardized by the hostilities between his nation and Great Britain. He needed the cooperation of American and British officials. Yet he knew that he was unlikely to find any enthusiasm for joint trading ventures between the two nations in a time of war.

After returning to the United States in April 1812, Cuffe was accused of breaking American trade regulations, and his ship and cargo were impounded. He then traveled to Washington, D.C. (shown here as it appeared in the early 1800s), to seek exoneration from the charge from President James Madison.

Nevertheless, Cuffe was still feeling confident that he had established the basis of an African trade network as he glimpsed the coast of New England. He sent his ship and crew to dock at New Bedford and hurried by boat to Westport to greet his family. He reached home on April 19. "Found my family well," he wrote. "In 30 minutes after we got in the harbor we had a very hard thunder squall. I felt thankful that I had so nicely escaped."

Cuffe may have escaped the storm, but the *Traveller* had not escaped the patrols of American navy ships. The morning after he returned home, he traveled to New Bedford to meet his ship and found, to his consternation, that it had been seized by American customs officials. He was informed that he had violated U.S. regulations by carrying cargo from a British colony, and his ship was towed to the local customs bureau at Newport, Rhode Island.

Cuffe had not been aware that Congress had recently passed a law banning all trade with Great Britain. The customs officials told him that his ignorance of the law did not matter and refused to return his ship and cargo to him. The only way he could get them back was by persuading Albert Gallatin, the U.S. secretary of the treasury, to exclude his cargo from the trade restrictions.

Cuffe's friends, including Rhode Island governor Simeon Martin and some other men of influence, immediately began a campaign to free the *Traveller* and its contents. Acting on their advice, Cuffe gathered his letters of recommendation, packed a suitcase, and took a coach to Washington, D.C. He carried with him a petition for the release of his ship that he hoped to present to both Gallatin and President James Madison.

Cuffe's journey to the nation's capital was pleasant, except for one incident at an inn. He was told by the innkeeper that he must sit at a table with the black servants if he wanted to dine there. Cuffe wrote of the encounter, "I told him as I rode with the company, I could eat with them." He sat down with his fellow travelers, and nothing more was said about the matter.

Cuffe arrived in Washington on a rainy morning in May 1812. The young city was still in a fairly raw state, and congressmen had to walk on muddy streets to attend the sessions at which they discussed the nation's preparations for war with Britain. Cuffe, fatigued from his trip, rested at the house of a Quaker friend named Samuel Hutchinson.

In Cuffe's time, American citizens did not need a formal appointment to meet with the president;

President James Madison gave Cuffe a warm reception when the black sea captain visited the White House on May 2, 1812. The president advocated the gradual abolition of slavery and the resettlement of free blacks in another country, and he was interested in Cuffe's efforts to found a homeland in Africa for black Americans.

they simply waited in line at his office. The day after Cuffe's arrival in the nation's capital, he and Hutchinson decided to call on the president and the secretary of the treasury. Madison had already received a number of letters of recommendation from Cuffe's friends, and he was sympathetic to the captain's cause.

When Cuffe met with Madison and told him about his business success in Africa, the president seemed impressed. He also expressed interest in Cuffe's ideas about establishing an African trading network, for he supported the efforts to resettle America's free black population in Africa. As for Cuffe's problems with Newport's customs officials, the president promised to do what he could to correct the situation.

Two days later, Cuffe met with Gallatin, who also greeted him warmly. Gallatin assured Cuffe that the *Traveller* would be returned to him and that all charges against him would be dropped. The secretary issued a statement that said, "It doth appear to my satisfaction that the voyage was not only innocent but was undertaken for most laudable and benevolent purposes." Gallatin then told Cuffe that the American government was prepared to assist his efforts to establish colonies in Africa and would be eager to hear any ideas he had for taking more forceful measures against the transatlantic slave trade. Cuffe, who insisted that he must continue "traveling in a path of peacefulness," told the secretary that Africa needed teachers rather than soldiers to rid the seas of slave ships.

When the elated Cuffe left Washington on May 5, 1812, his reputation as a leading authority on African affairs was firmly established. His meetings with Madison and Gallatin had convinced him that he could count on the support of the nation's highest officials for his African colonization efforts. Grateful

During Cuffe's visit to the nation's capital, Secretary of the Treasury Albert Gallatin presented the black sea captain with the documents that released him from all charges filed against him by the U.S. customs department. The secretary also promised government assistance for Cuffe's African trade venture.

for the president's help and encouragement, he wrote a letter of thanks to Madison, concluding it with a wish that "the blessings of heaven attend thee."

The high spirits that Cuffe took with him from the capital did not last for long. On one leg of the trip home, a bewigged and bigoted fellow traveler whom Cuffe described as a "bustling powder-headed man" berated him for taking the most comfortable seat in the coach. The man was obviously hoping that Cuffe would leave the coach. But Cuffe refused to move, even in the face of more taunts. After a few tense minutes, a woman and a young girl appeared in the coach doorway, and Cuffe quickly rose. "We always give way to accommodate the women," he stated, taking another seat.

FEDERAL GAZETTE:

THURSDAY.....MAY 7.

PAUL CUFFEE, captain and owner of the brig Traveller, is now in town. This is the coloured man of whom some account was lately published from an English paper. His vessel and cargo were seized at Newport, R.I. on his return from Sierra Leone, in Africa.—Captain C. had been 18 months absent, and was unacquainted with the *grabbing* and *restrictive* practices of his native country. He went to Washington—and having stated his case to government, was very politely treated, and his vessel and cargo immediately restored. This pious and humane citizen has already been of considerable service to many of the Africans, to whom he has carried several teachers—and for whose further benefit he appears willing to employ many of his days and much of his large pecuniary resources.

THE FRENCH.—We wish it to be explicitly understood, as our opinion, that there is no room for *doubt* as to the existence of the French decrees, which the President *says* are off. As some people, however, believe only what Democrats say, we republish the following confessions from the democratic papers of this city.

From the " Whig "

FRENCH AGGRESSION, &c.

The capture of the ship Congress, (owned by major Biays) on her voyage hence for England, by a French vessel, augurs badly. She was not laden with any article which under the treaty with France of '78 or of 1800 can be deemed contraband of war. She was freighted with the produce of our own soil, flour, tobacco, tar, turpentine, &c. If France does not make speedy reparation for this and other spoliations on " our lawful commerce," we had better prepare to rescind all commercial intercourse with her.

Newspapers throughout the country—including the Federal Gazette—*printed stories about Cuffe's meeting with President Madison. Cuffe's African emigration campaign thus received extensive national publicity.*

To Cuffe's amusement and amazement, the "powder-headed" man's behavior toward him later made a complete turnaround because of a chance meeting between Cuffe and Rhode Island senator William Hunter at a travelers' rest stop. The senator, who had supported Cuffe's quest to regain his ship, greeted the captain and wished him well. Seeing this encounter, Cuffe's fellow traveler became friendly and began to address him as "Captain."

Cuffe's resolution was again tested in Baltimore, at a tavern where he stopped for dinner. He was told by the owner that he would have to eat in the back with the servants, and he flatly refused. "Not as I thought myself better than the servants," he later wrote, "but from the nature of the cause." He immediately found another tavern where the proprietor had no segregationist rules.

While in Baltimore, Cuffe discovered that his name was becoming well known. Some of the local newspapers had printed accounts of his meeting with President Madison. He capitalized on his growing reputation by meeting with many of the city's prominent free black citizens and abolitionist leaders, and he urged them to help him find families who were interested in emigrating to Africa.

Cuffe also stopped in Philadelphia on his journey home, to rouse support for his African venture. Much of the city's black community turned out to hear him speak about his experiences in Africa. Later, he met with his friends Benjamin Rush, Absalom Jones, and James Forten, who talked with him about their efforts to abolish slavery.

By the time Cuffe reached New York, his fame had reached sizable proportions. He was greeted there by a crowd of well-wishers and ushered to a black schoolhouse, where he once more discussed his travels to Sierra Leone. After hearing Cuffe speak, a group of prominent blacks and Quakers agreed to join his

supporters in other cities to form an organization that would assist his efforts in Africa.

While in New York, Cuffe met a doctor who had moved back to America after living in Jamaica for seven years. The doctor told him horrifying stories about life on the island's sugar plantations, where slaves were commonly whipped, mutilated, and burned alive. After hearing these stories, Cuffe was thoroughly unamused when two white clergymen who apparently had a low opinion of black intelligence stopped him in the street and asked if he understood English. He responded that "there was a part I did not understand, that of one brother . . . holding in bondage his brother." Taken aback by this reply, the ministers hurried away.

Upon leaving New York, Cuffe traveled to Newport, where he presented the customs officials with the documents that permitted him to regain possession of his beloved *Traveller*. Once more at the helm

Cuffe reported that he found "friends on every side" during his coach ride home from Washington, D.C. Most notably, he was greeted as a conquering hero by black and Quaker groups in Philadelphia and New York City, where he drew large audiences for his lectures on Africa.

An American ship (foreground) races for safety as a British vessel gives chase during the War of 1812. Cuffe had to postpone his planned voyage to Sierra Leone after Congress denied him permission to trade with Britain's African colony.

of his ship, he sailed proudly into Westport harbor, arriving there in the middle of May. He made trips to nearby towns in the following weeks to arrange for the sale of his cargo of English fabrics, African animal hides, and peanuts.

By the summer of 1812, Cuffe had settled down to life in Westport and began to attend to long-neglected business matters. While Britain and the United States remained at war, there was little he could do about making firm plans for his next voyage to Sierra Leone. But he was determined to keep the idea of emigration to Africa alive in the minds of black Americans. He knew that the war would have to end someday, and that he would then return to Africa. He hoped to be able to take with him a group of black settlers who were willing to brave the wilds of Africa for the chance to build a free and prosperous home in the land of their ancestors. With a group of dedicated pioneers to serve as teachers and Christian missionaries to the African natives, he felt sure that the hated slave trade could at last be stamped out.

In preparation for his next trip overseas, Cuffe wrote often to black church and social organizations throughout America to encourage them to think about Africa. Enthusiasm for his plans was especially great in Boston, where a large number of volunteers stated that they were ready to join his next expedition. He also kept up his correspondence with the directors of the African Institution in London and the members of the Friendly Society of Sierra Leone. He wrote to his British friend William Allen: "Notwithstanding the declaration of war between these two countries, I hope that chain of brotherly union in the true church is not shortened." Allen assured him that the African Institution was still eager to work with him.

When Cuffe was not working on business matters or the planning of his next voyage, he was busy helping to improve the local community. In 1813—15 years after he had built a schoolhouse in Westport— he paid for half the cost of building a new Quaker meetinghouse. This time all the local members of the Society of Friends pitched in to help raise the structure.

Cuffe managed to remain in the public eye while his next expedition to Africa remained on hold. The *Weekly Messenger*, a Boston newspaper, published a seven-part article about him entitled "Paul Cuffe's Mission to Sierra Leone." At the same time, another account of his life, a pamphlet entitled *Memoirs of Captain Paul Cuffee*, was being distributed by abolitionist societies.

As the War of 1812 dragged on into 1814, Cuffe began to grow impatient. At the age of 55, he could no longer afford to wait for his opportunities. The idea of asking Congress for special permission to sail to Sierra Leone had been growing in his mind, and at last he decided to put his plan into action.

More than 30 years earlier, Cuffe and his brother John had sent a petition to their county legislature concerning the issue of taxation without government

When the Americans and British signed a peace treaty early in 1815, Cuffe once more made preparations for a trip to Africa. His ship's bill of lading for the voyage listed nails, hoes, soap, shoes, a wagon, and other items that were needed by the settlers in Sierra Leone.

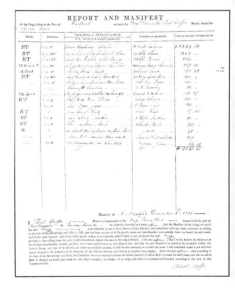

Cuffe's announcement that he would be taking a shipload of settlers to Africa at the end of 1815 aroused a great deal of excitement in black communities throughout America. James Forten, the owner of a sail-making business in Philadelphia, was the president of one group that applauded Cuffe's "benevolent undertaking."

representation. At that time, he had been a little-known boat owner, and his petition had been denied. Now, with friends and supporters in the highest ranks of government, he felt confident that he would succeed in getting permission from Congress to carry on with his African trading venture.

Cuffe wrote to William Allen in England and asked him to arrange it with British officials so he could travel to Sierra Leone. Then he drew up a petition to his own government. He sent the document to Senator Christopher Gore and Congressman Leban Wheaton of Massachusetts. On January 7, 1814, they submitted the petition to the president and both houses of Congress.

Cuffe's document aroused such interest in the nation's capital that it was printed in the town's leading newspapers. He asserted in the petition that the object of his mission was "to promote the improvement and civilization of Africa." He discussed his ideas for building a trade network with Africa and for fighting the slave trade through economic measures. Emphasizing that his plans were founded on Christian charity, he stated that as a businessmen he still needed to be granted the right to trade with the British in order to pay for his humanitarian work and to help black families emigrate to Africa.

Cuffe's petition was transformed into a bill and was quickly passed by the Senate. In the House of Representatives, however, the bill ran into stiff resistance. Critics of Cuffe's plan charged that the black captain's idea of establishing trade with a struggling colony of the British enemy was not only unpatriotic but also a foolish business venture. Disturbing racial questions also entered the debate, for many of the supporters of Cuffe's petition were slaveholders who were interested in founding an organization that would force free blacks to resettle in Africa. These men believed that they could weaken the abolitionist movement if they could eliminate the militant free black population.

In March 1814, the bill was defeated by a small margin in the House of Representatives, thus ending Cuffe's hopes of sailing to Africa while the war still raged. Disappointed, he returned to his family and business affairs and spent whatever time he could teaching young men in Westport the skills of navigation. A born teacher, he was generous in sharing his knowledge of sailing, trading, and farming, and he always had lively stories to tell about dangerous storms at sea and about life in Africa. Nevertheless, he was impatient to put his navigational skills to work by sailing to Africa once more.

The long-awaited news finally came on December 24, 1814: The United States and Great Britain had signed a peace treaty. Cuffe immediately began to make arrangements for his next trip to Africa. He already had a sizable list of people who wanted to sail with him, and his Westport farm became active once more as supplies and trade goods were gathered for the upcoming voyage. His cargo included hoes, a wagon, building materials for a sawmill, and other items that would be useful to American settlers in Africa.

By the end of 1815, the preparations were complete. On December 4, Cuffe wrote to William Allen, "I shall sail, through God's permission, the first wind after tomorrow." ⚓

8
"RISE TO BE A PEOPLE"

Cuffe's SECOND VOYAGE from America to Sierra Leone began on December 10, 1815. As he piloted the *Traveller* out of Westport, he felt both excited and worried. Much of his life's savings was invested in the voyage, on which the future of his proposed African trading network was resting, and he was uncertain about what type of welcome he would receive when he reached Freetown. William Allen had not been able to assure him that his trading license in the colony would be renewed.

On board the *Traveller* were 38 passengers whom Cuffe hoped would be the first group of a legion of black American pioneers in Africa. Each of the families in the group had been recommended to him by respected clergymen, and he was providing free passage for all but eight of the settlers. Most of them were experienced farmers who knew how to cultivate tobacco and other crops that could be planted in Sierra Leone. The unofficial leader of the group was a Boston minister named Perry Lockes, whom Cuffe described affectionately as having "rather a hard voice for a preacher."

Lockes's invigorating sermons were needed on the tempestuous voyage across the ocean. Cuffe wrote

Early in 1816, Cuffe made his third entry into Freetown harbor, this time delivering 38 homesteaders onto African soil.

95

Cuffe's logbook records the names and ages of the Traveller's *passengers on the 1815 voyage to Africa. The British gave each of the nine American settler families a plot of land in Sierra Leone, although Cuffe himself was allowed to carry out only limited trading in the colony.*

that for 3 particularly storm-filled weeks, the ship's passengers "experienced 20 days of the most tremendous weather that I remember." For almost half the journey, the Atlantic's winter gales assaulted the *Traveller*, battering the sails with icy winds and sweeping the deck with rain and monstrous waves. Finally, the storms died down. But then almost all the passengers and crew fell ill from seasickness. Cuffe was one of the few to remain on his feet and help nurse the others through their illness.

The *Traveller*'s crew and passengers were greatly relieved when they finally saw the mountains of Sierra Leone looming in the distance. However, the initial reaction of Freetown's officials to the arrival of the American ship was enough to dampen much of the passengers' enthusiasm for the colony. Cuffe was told that his ship would be allowed only a few hours in port, an order that was grudgingly changed after he explained that he had many passengers on board.

The next two months were a frustrating period for Cuffe as he battled to overcome British restrictions on American trading vessels. After meeting with Charles MacCarthy, the new colonial governor, he was able to win official assurance that each of the American families on the *Traveller* would be given a plot of land to farm. He was less successful at gaining any concessions for himself. His cargo was taxed at an excessive rate, and he was allowed to charge only a small price for his goods. Having already spent a considerable amount on transporting his passengers to Africa, he now faced a severe financial loss. Despondent, he wrote to his friend William Rotch, "If nothing favorable appears in a few days I shall leave Sierra Leone for America."

But Cuffe remained at Sierra Leone and resumed the work he had begun earlier to make Freetown a prosperous port. In association with the Friendly Society, he began to form plans for a factory to be built inland. This industrial center would, he hoped, provide jobs for the local native population and help lessen their dependence on the profits of the slave trade. His other plans included the building of a sawmill and a rice mill and the development of a tobacco-growing industry.

Cuffe was pleased to see that the Friendly Society of Sierra Leone was thriving despite attempts by Freetown's white merchants to limit the business opportunities of the black community. There were other hopeful signs. During his time in Sierra Leone, he saw that the families he had brought to the colony were already beginning to play an important role in fostering agriculture and trade.

The Americans had some trouble accepting some of the civic responsibilities that the settlers in Sierra Leone were expected to perform. Cuffe heard Perry Lockes complain that he had to take time from his work to serve on a jury. "I told him he complained in America because he was deprived of these liberties," said Cuffe, and he told the preacher to be happy about his opportunity to serve the community. Lockes eventually became a respected leader of the Freetown settlers.

Despite his troubles with Sierra Leone's administration, Cuffe was still confident that the colony could become the center of an African trading network. But his latest voyage to the colony had exhausted his financial resources. He knew he had to return immediately to the United States so he could start restoring his fortune.

On April 4, 1816, Cuffe said good-bye to his friends in Sierra Leone and sailed from Freetown. As he waved to a crowd gathered at the dock to see him off, he realized how much he had come to love Africa—the land of his father and the future home, he hoped, of the oppressed black population of America. He planned to return to Sierra Leone the following

year if he could arrange more favorable trading terms with the British.

Cuffe again sailed the *Traveller* across the Atlantic and docked in New York in late May. Instead of resting from his travels, he immediately aroused some controversy in the city by launching a personal campaign against the illegal transatlantic slave trade. Speaking at a meeting held by a black social group, he reported the names of prominent local white businessmen who were the owners of slave ships. He had discovered this information from British officials in Africa. Newspapers in many cities printed Cuffe's list and congratulated him for his courageous attack on the slave traders.

Back in Westport with his family, Cuffe discovered that his recent spell of financial bad luck had not changed. The New England economy was in a temporary depression when he returned home, and

During Cuffe's third visit to Sierra Leone, he and the members of the Friendly Society discussed plans for building mills and factories around Freetown. Cuffe hoped that the proposed enterprises would be the forerunners of a surge of black-owned business operations in Africa.

he had a difficult time selling the lumber he had brought back from his last trip to Sierra Leone.

By this time, the *Traveller* was the only ship in Cuffe's fleet. The others either had been sold or had been scrapped due to old age. Realizing that he could not finance another expedition to Africa, Cuffe instead kept his ship busy hauling cargoes along the East Coast during 1816 and 1817.

Cuffe did not abandon his efforts to establish the trade route with Africa during this period. The British, however, refused to grant him a license for special trading rights in Sierra Leone, and none of the American business or philanthropic organizations he consulted were willing to take on the costly financial burden of sponsoring African colonization efforts. To the settler Perry Lockes, who inquired in 1816 when the *Traveller*'s captain would complete his arrangements for his next visit to Freetown, Cuffe wrote, "I fancy all this will not be brought about in time to come to Sierra Leone until another year."

Cuffe was more certain about another matter: the urgency of creating an African homeland for black Americans. Whatever hopes he had harbored that some degree of racial equality could be achieved in his country were fast disappearing. The year 1816 was marked by a heightening of racial tensions throughout America. In the South, rumors circulated that slave rebellions were being planned, and many whites feared a revolt on the scale of the one that had driven the French from Haiti more than a decade before. The spread of slavery seemed destined to continue, but many people had begun to believe that a day of reckoning was fast approaching for America.

Cuffe could not understand why the slave owners could not free their slaves and allow them to live with dignity and freedom in America or Africa. White Americans, he said, "are preparing instruments for their own execution." In a similar vein, when he heard about the wreck of a slave ship called the *Princess Charlotte* with the loss of everyone on board, he stated, "God will not always suffer the wicked to go unpunished."

Stalled in his attempts to organize a black exodus from America, the weary Cuffe could only pray that someone else would step forward to carry on his work. He urged members of the Friendly Society of Sierra Leone to form new commercial outposts in Africa that would grow and become, he said, "known among the Nations of the Earth." Writing to black communities in America, he exhorted them to remember Africa, the only place, he said, where blacks could "rise to be a people."

There was a story about black nationalism that Cuffe liked to relate to young people at Quaker meetings. One night when he was 12, he said, he went on an errand alone. Walking through the darkness,

he grew afraid that he might be attacked by a wild animal. So he bent over a fence that marked the outer border of his father's land and picked up a stick that looked like what he needed. Once he had the stick in his hand, however, he realized that he had no right to it since he had taken it from his neighbor's property. A stolen weapon, he believed, would be of no use in defending himself.

Tossing the stick away, Cuffe searched his father's land until he found a suitable piece of wood. "It proved to be a club," he told his listeners, adding that he picked up the stick and carried it with him as he went cheerfully on his way. Just as he could not feel secure carrying a stick from his neighbor's property, so, he said, blacks could be content only if they lived in a land of their own.

Emaciated Africans lie in the hold of a captured slave ship. Cuffe gathered information in Sierra Leone about American merchants still participating in the outlawed slave trade, and after returning to the United States in 1816, he used the national press to launch a public attack on the culprits.

In late 1816, Cuffe was contacted by a group of white southerners who said they were interested in providing black Americans with their own land. These men, many of whom shared the same racist sentiments expressed by the slaveholding congressmen who had supported Cuffe's petition, were members of a newly formed organization called the American Colonization Society. Their goal was to fund efforts to resettle free blacks and manumitted slaves in a colony in Africa. The society's members were well aware of Cuffe's efforts to spur emigration to Africa, and they hoped that he would support their work.

Cuffe was somewhat leery of the American Colonization Society's motives, yet he welcomed the efforts of the well-financed organization to promote emigration to Africa. The society's founder, the Reverend Robert Finley, was clearly sympathetic to the suffering of blacks in America, and the organization enjoyed the support of President James Monroe. The white colonizers' plans seemed to dovetail well with

The American Colonization Society, an organization composed of white southerners, shared Cuffe's goal of resettling free blacks in Africa. Although he initially welcomed the colonizers' support, Cuffe changed his opinion after deciding their program was designed for the interests of slaveholders and was not for "the benefit of the African Nation."

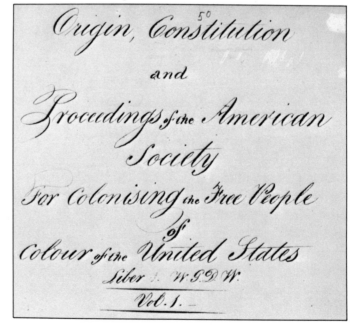

Cuffe's own, and as the captain read through the stack of applications he had received from would-be colonists, he realized that many ships would be needed to carry all who wished to move to Africa.

Cuffe had been promoting the idea of African colonization for a long time, but he had been slow to realize that Africa could receive only a trickle of those who wanted to move to a black homeland. Perhaps, he decided, "as it is not at all likely all may be prevailed on to emigrate to Africa," a black colony should be created in America as well. In the last months of 1816, he sent a petition to the legislature of New Jersey, asking it to provide funds for a colony on the coast of Africa "or elsewhere," so that the state's black citizens could live free of racial prejudice. The legislators endorsed his idea of founding a colony in Africa, but they were unwilling to discuss the idea of creating a separate black state in America.

By the beginning of 1817, Cuffe's health was beginning to fail. Nevertheless, he forged ahead with his efforts to promote black migration to Africa. All the while, he gradually distanced himself from the American Colonization Society, whose racist attitudes were becoming ever more clear to him and other blacks. The society's directors, most of whom were slaveholders, appeared to be far more interested in upholding the slave system and eliminating the country's free black population than in helping blacks establish a home for themselves. The organization stirred up great resentment in the black community, and in Philadelphia, James Forten and Richard Allen conducted public meetings at which the society's plans were condemned.

As his health continued to fail, Cuffe realized that his part in national affairs was almost at an end. He remained at his farm in Westport and enjoyed the visits of his many friends and family members. But he felt his strength continuing to slip away, and his

The Reverend Richard Allen, who supported Cuffe's efforts to found a homeland in Africa for black Americans, was a savage critic of the American Colonization Society. He called the organization an "outrage" and accused it of trying to drive free blacks from the United States while helping to strengthen slavery's hold in the South.

thoughts turned more and more to his own mortality. "No age, nation . . . in whatever part of the world are exempt from death's summons," he wrote.

On September 7, 1817, a dying Cuffe told those who sat at his bedside that the afterworld was a celestial city whose streets were paved with transparent glass and pearls. He added, "Let me pass quietly away," and then he died. He was 58 years old, and he left to his wife and children the considerable fortune that he had managed to rebuild.

Cuffe's dream of founding a homeland in Africa for black Americans was only partially fulfilled in the decades following his death. No one of comparable stature emerged to lead an exodus of blacks to Africa, although some blacks participated in the American Colonization Society's controversial effort in the early 1820s to found a colony to the south of Sierra Leone. In 1847, this tiny colony became the nation of Liberia, the first black republic to be established in Africa.

Most black Americans, though, did not leave the United States. They remained in bondage until a mounting antislavery movement helped start a civil war that brought about an end to slavery in the 1860s. Yet racial oppression continues to exist in the United States more than a century later, despite the efforts of black activists from all walks of American life.

Few people, however, have traveled as far as Cuffe in the name of black freedom. Imbued with a nobility of character that impressed almost everyone who knew him, he championed the rights of black Americans at a time when only a few lonely voices dared to speak out. Throughout his life, he was battered, it seems, as much by the storms of human injustice as by the forces of nature. Yet he refused to let any obstacles deter him in his quest for a black homeland. A man of daring and determination, the sea captain from Westport always believed that the land of liberty was never far away. It was just over the horizon. ✺

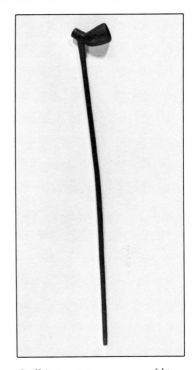

Cuffe's iron pipe was one of his comforts during his last days, which he spent at his farm in Westport. He was hailed at the time of his death as a daring pioneer whose voyages helped to build a bridge from America to Africa.

The navigator's compass used by Cuffe.

CHRONOLOGY

1759	Born Paul Cuffe on Cuttyhunk Island, Massachusetts
1766	Moves to Westport, Massachusetts
1772	Cuffe's father dies
1773	Joins the crew of a whaling vessel
1776	Held briefly as British prisoner of war during the American Revolution
1779	Begins small trading operation along New England coast
1780	Petitions county legislature to end taxation without representation for blacks
1783	Marries Alice Pequit
1784	Expands shipping company and builds first ships in his own shipyard
1797	Establishes public school in Westport
1803	Expands trade network to Europe
1808	Joins the Society of Friends and begins abolitionist work
1810–11	Makes first voyage to Sierra Leone and begins attempt to establish a trade network between America and Africa; also visits England
1812	Travels to Washington, D.C., and meets with President Madison
1814	Petitions Congress for special trading privileges during the War of 1812
1815	Transports American settlers to Africa on last voyage to Sierra Leone
1817	Dies at his farm in Westport on September 17

FURTHER READING

Atkin, Mary Gage. *Paul Cuffe and the African Promised Land.* New York: Thomas Nelson, 1977.

Franklin, John Hope. *From Slavery to Freedom: A History of Negro Americans.* New York: Knopf, 1980.

Green, Lorenzo J. *The Negro in Colonial New England.* New York: Atheneum, 1969.

Harris, Sheldon H. *Paul Cuffe: Black America and the African Return.* New York: Simon & Schuster, 1972.

Johnston, Johanna. *Paul Cuffee: America's First Black Captain.* New York: Dodd, Mead, 1970.

Meier, August, and Elliot Rudwick, eds. *The Making of Black America.* New York: Atheneum, 1969.

Peterson, John. *Province of Freedom: A History of Sierra Leone, 1787–1870.* Evanston, IL: Northwestern University Press, 1969.

Salvador, George Arnold. *Paul Cuffe, the Black Yankee, 1759–1817.* New Bedford, MA: Reynolds-Dewalt Printing, 1969.

Thomas, Lamont. *Paul Cuffe: Black Entrepreneur and Pan-Africanist.* Urbana: University of Illinois Press, 1986.

West, Richard. *Back to Africa: A History of Sierra Leone and Liberia.* New York: Holt, Rinehart and Winston, 1970.

INDEX

PICTURE CREDITS

ARTHUR DIAMOND was born in Queens, New York, and has lived and worked in New Mexico, Colorado, and Oregon. He holds a bachelor's degree in English from the University of Oregon and is currently working on a master's degree in English at Queens College. A book editor in New York City, he is the author of *The Romanian Americans* in the PEOPLES OF NORTH AMERICA series published by Chelsea House.

NATHAN IRVIN HUGGINS is W.E.B. Du Bois Professor of History and Director of the W.E.B. Du Bois Institute for Afro-American Research at Harvard University. He previously taught at Columbia University. Professor Huggins is the author of numerous books, including *Black Odyssey: The Afro-American Ordeal in Slavery, The Harlem Renaissance,* and *Slave and Citizen: The Life of Frederick Douglass.*